Table of Contents

D0121882

A Note from Chuck Swindoll

The world has lost its way.

More than ever, in the morass and the chaos of our times, the people of God need a clear vision of our role as God's servants on earth. Our modern world offers increasingly diverse choices when it comes to answering our biggest questions. But as wave after wave of options roll over us, people are more confused than ever before.

As followers of Christ, we know to seek direction and guidance from the Scriptures. However, the original Deceiver—Satan himself—has infiltrated every corner of this world. Many come on his behalf, with Bibles in hand, speaking lies and deception in the name of Jesus Christ. Christians need to be on the alert for deceivers waiting to trip us up, both out in the world and inside the stained-glass confines of the church. If we mean to persevere to the end in our Christian lives, it's imperative that we understand the world in which we live and the response to deception that God expects of us.

To that end, I've contributed two chapters to begin this book. The first describes our changing times and the biblical illiteracy that has stymied the church in its response to the world. Let's be honest; we simply haven't done a good enough job passing on the knowledge and wisdom from the Scriptures to the next generation. We need a wholesale recommitment to God and His Word. The second chapter takes a hard look at the presence of deception in the world and among Christians. If we hope to impact the world for Christ, we must understand the nature of deceivers, the message they peddle, and the proper response Christians should have to error.

After those first two chapters, we asked several writers (most of whom serve at Stonebriar Community Church, the church I pastor in Frisco, Texas) to contribute study chapters relating to the age group or segment of society to which they minister. From fifth and sixth grade kids on up to professional adults, these chapters walk you through the minefield of culture and deception in a way that applies to you and your children. Digest each of these chapters, even if they don't necessarily fit your specific situation in life. You will find much to appreciate and to apply.

Wherever you are and however you shine the light of Christ into this dark world, the ideas in this book will provide a reliable guide for you, pointing you back to God's Word as the cornerstone of your authority.

Sure, the world has lost its way . . . but let's not forget: we have been found.

Chuck Swindoll

Charles R. Swindoll

How to Use This Study

In our troubled times, we can find much to lament—an increase in violence, injustice all over the world, and abortions on demand. The list goes on. As believers in the true God, we can take solace in the hope our faith provides, but that doesn't always make living in this world an easy proposition.

Hope for Our Troubled Times offers you a unique perspective—wisdom about life in this world directly from Chuck Swindoll, along with a series of study chapters written by pastors and Christian leaders who are on the front lines of ministry every day. You'll find two chapters from Chuck to begin the book. These will set the stage, pinpointing some of the problems with deception that our world faces and delivering guidance from the Bible on how to deal with the deceivers in our lives.

Beginning with chapter 3, you will find seven study chapters written for a variety of ages and groups—from a chapter directed to the parents of fifth and sixth graders to one directed to those living as single adults in our troubled world. You are sure to find at least a couple of study chapters that fit your particular situation. And, because each chapter provides a unique take on responding to the deceptions of our world, you may find it helpful to review every chapter.

You may choose to work through this study individually or with a group, but regardless of how you choose to complete this study, a brief introduction to the overall structure of each study chapter (3–9) will help you get the most out of it.

Study Chapter Organization

 THE HEART OF THE MATTER highlights the main idea of each chapter for general orientation. The chapter itself is then composed of two main teaching sections for insight and application:

 DISCOVERING THE WAY explores the principles of Scripture, drawing out practical tools for life. Parallel passages and additional questions supplement the main Scriptures for a more in-depth study.

 STARTING YOUR JOURNEY focuses on application, helping you to put into practice the principles of the chapter in ways that fit your personality, gifts, and level of spiritual maturity.

Using *Hope for Our Troubled Times* Study Chapters

Hope for Our Troubled Times is designed with individual study in mind, but it may be adapted for group study. If you choose to use this study in a group setting, please keep in mind that many of the study chapters ask personal, probing questions, seeking to elicit answers that reveal an individual's true character and challenge the reader to change. Therefore, the answers to some of the questions in this book may be potentially embarrassing if they are shared in a group setting. Care, therefore, should be taken by the group leader to prepare the group for the sensitive nature of these studies, to forgo certain questions if they appear to be too personal, and to remain perceptive to the mood and dynamics of the group if questions or answers become uncomfortable.

Whether you use this book in groups or individually, we recommend the following method:

Prayer—Begin each study chapter with prayer, asking God to teach you through His Word and to open your heart to the self-discovery afforded by the questions and text of the chapter.

Scripture—Have your Bible handy. We recommend the
New American Standard Bible or another literal translation, rather
than a paraphrase. As you progress through each study chapter, you'll
be prompted to read relevant sections of Scripture and answer questions related to the topic. You will also want to look up the Scripture
passages noted in parentheses. We have added an "a" or "b" to some
of the references, pointing you to the first or second half of a verse,
rather than to the entire verse.

Questions—As you encounter the questions, approach them
wisely and creatively. Not every question will be applicable to each
person all the time. Use the questions as general guides in your thinking rather than rigid forms to complete. If there are things you just
don't understand or that you want to explore further, be sure to jot
down your thoughts or questions.

Our prayer is that this book will not only help you face the
realities of our world with God's truth but also provide insights and
application for your day-to-day life.

HOPE
for Our Troubled
TIMES

Chapter One

The Disturbing Realities of Our Times
by Charles R. Swindoll

Don't you just sometimes shake your head and wonder, *What on earth is happening in the world?* We've come upon tough times, to be sure. These days, we immediately think of the economy. Our minds may also drift to other topics: greedy Wall Street brokers, lying politicians, or a lack of trust in authority, to name a few. However, the disturbing realities of our times go much deeper than a weak housing market or a lost job, serious as those may be.

Of utmost importance to the well-informed Christian is the insidious and expansive cultural erosion of our times. So subtle and so extensive is the problem, we find it almost impossible to get our arms around. Wise and attentive believers should not be surprised that our culture has lost its way and its values have spiraled downward.

Jesus Himself, during His earthly ministry, predicted such times as these. He told His disciples there would be days of tribulation. Many would fall away. He warned of betrayal, hatred, murder, and vice. He stated that lawlessness would not only occur; it would increase. He cautioned that many false prophets would arise and that most people's love would grow cold (Matthew 24:9–12). Isn't this a picture of the world we live in today—fractured, unhinged, and chaotic?

As Jesus left the earth and passed on the torch of responsibility to His apostles, they ran with it. They spoke boldly. They wrote forcefully, and none more so than the apostle Paul. In writing to Timothy, Paul's young friend, I can imagine Paul's pen pressing harder into the parchment as he warned Timothy, "The Spirit makes it clear that as time goes on, some are going to give up on the faith and chase after demonic illusions put forth by professional liars" (1 Timothy 4:1 MSG). What a statement! Later, just before Paul was martyred, he wrote again to Timothy,

> Don't be naive. There are difficult times ahead. As the end approaches, people are going to be self-absorbed, money-hungry, self-promoting, stuck-up, profane, contemptuous of parents, crude, coarse, dog-eat-dog, unbending, slanderers, impulsively wild, savage, cynical, treacherous, ruthless, bloated windbags, addicted to lust, and allergic to God. (2 Timothy 3:1–5 MSG)

This list stands as a litany of our times. Should it surprise us, then, when we read what we read, see what we see, and hear what we hear on a daily basis? We've come upon tough times.

Analyzing the World

Obviously, the first-century writers of Scripture had an accurate picture of how this world would end up. By the inspiration of God's Holy Spirit, they pinpointed the evils of men and women all over the earth. But they also wrote of our response to the times. They knew believers would struggle to live and minister amid rampant sin and shame. The biblical authors faced similar trials themselves! Read carefully the words of the apostle John in his first epistle:

> Do not love the world nor the things in the world. If anyone loves the world, the love of the Father is not in him. For all that is in the world, the lust of the flesh and the lust of the eyes and the boastful pride of life, is not from the Father, but is from the world. The world is passing away, and also its lusts; but the one who does the will of God lives forever. (1 John 2:15–17)

2

When John the apostle wrote, "Do not love the world nor the things in the world," he truly understood what our times would be like. As one of the original twelve disciples, he had heard the warnings and predictions spoken by Jesus Himself. And living as a Christian in the middle of the Roman Empire, he would have seen the evidence of sin all around him.

Six times in these three verses, John used the Greek term *cosmos*. The word refers to the world's system, which is headed by Satan. As a result, the world has no interest in following the true God and carries an outwardly hostile attitude toward Christ and Holy Scripture. These attitudes characterize our times. They dictate much of what we see on television, hear on the radio, and read online. So, through John, God commands believers not to give our love to this world—a constant struggle because everyone who has ever lived lives in that same world!

Now, you know I am not a witch hunter. I don't see the Devil behind every bush. But you also need to know there is a conspiracy going on. Greater powers than humanity continue to wage an invisible war (Ephesians 6:11–12). If you don't understand that, you will be hopelessly confused and frustrated by the onslaught of unbiblical ideas that come with living in this fallen world. We have to learn to see the world through the lens of Scripture.

Defining "Many Antichrists"

Under God's permissive will, this world runs its wicked course filled with the lust of the flesh, the lust of the eyes, and the boastful pride of life. All of this occurs under the influence of the one whom God allows to have his way for a short time: Satan.

John wrote that "it is the last hour; and just as you heard that antichrist is coming . . . " (1 John 2:18). Stop right there a moment. I believe this "antichrist" refers to a real individual—a powerful, persuasive, tyrannical, brutal, and brilliant individual—who will hold out empty words of hope to the gullible, sign a peace treaty in the Middle East to settle that incessant conflict, and suck under his influence the attention and the adoration of this naive world. Antichrist is coming.

All sorts of people have been suggested to fit into the identity of Antichrist. David Jeremiah, in a fine book titled *What in the World Is Going On?* wrote: "The very word *antichrist* sends a shudder through the hearts of Christians. All have heard or read of him . . . yet his identity is not revealed. . . . Many names have been suggested. When you google 'Who is Antichrist?' you get about 1.5 million hits."[1]

However, my major concern in this chapter is the ending of verse 18: "even now many antichrists have appeared; from this we know that it is the last hour" (1 John 2:18). John offered a similar sentiment in chapter 4 of this same letter: "every spirit that does not confess Jesus is not from God; this is the spirit of the antichrist, of which you have heard that it is coming, and now it is already in the world" (4:3). Rather than speculate about the identity of a future Antichrist, the church should consider those antichrists that have already appeared.

What does John mean by "many antichrists"? If we break up the word into its component parts, "anti" can mean one of two things—either "against" or "instead of." So the spirit of antichrist will be either a spirit that works against the person, work, and plan of Christ, or it could refer to counterfeit Christs, people who intend to stand in Christ's place. In this second sense, the word would refer to people who come on the scene offering answers, who are energized by the adversary who has his way and sway over this world. *Against* Christ or *instead of* Christ—either way, these pseudo-Christs, of which there are many, "have appeared" and "from this we know that it is the last hour" (2:18).

Understanding Our Times

For the balance of this chapter, I'd like to make you aware of the influence of these many antichrists. It's important we see what is occurring in the day in which we live—what is changing and where it seems to be leading. You and I both know the importance of understanding this erosion. We see marriages failing and homes in foreclosure. We notice that lying is on the ascent . . . and integrity is on the wane. We live in a world that's increasingly fearful, though it isn't always sure where to direct those fears. As believers in Jesus Christ, we must understand our times so that we can better understand our own identity and that of the world in which we hope to minister.

Sons and Daughters of Issachar

Before we analyze our times any further, let's examine a rather unknown — but very instructive — section of Scripture. First Chronicles 12 recounts Israel's days fighting for its existence under the leadership of David. As David led the people in battle, God raised up a body of men called the sons of Issachar. Look at their mini-biography: "Of the sons of Issachar, men who understood the times, with knowledge of what Israel should do, their chiefs were two hundred; and all their kinsmen were at their command" (1 Chronicles 12:32). This tribe of Hebrews exhibited courage on the battlefield and, as we shall see, discernment and decisiveness.

Steve Farrar paints a fine portrait of the men of Issachar in his book *Standing Tall*.

> These men had two things that made them a cut above the rest:
>
> • The men of Issachar had discernment.
> • The men of Issachar had direction.
>
> The men of Issachar saw what others didn't see. They looked behind the physical events and circumstances and realized there were spiritual forces influencing the conditions and situations of the nation from behind a parted curtain. That's why the men of Issachar were so valuable. . . . They had discernment. They could stare a hole right through the obvious and

see what wasn't obvious. Because of their discernment, they were then able to offer direction. . . .

. . . Because they understood their culture and the forces at work behind the scenes, they knew what Israel should do.[2]

I wish that we Christians would become sons and daughters of Issachar! I pray that God would cause a number of us to become people of discernment in our times, people with the courage to see what is really happening and then operate our lives based on what we know we ought to do. This would include any number of issues: the politics of our day, the spiritual apathy of our culture, and the directionless, hopeless, and immoral morass that the great majority of our world finds itself in today.

I hope, as the chapters of this book unfold, that you will gain some discernment in areas where you may have allowed your thoughts to slip into neutral. I hope you will put your mind back in gear so that you will be able to offer direction to those who have lost their way. It will not be simple. It is never easy to think for yourself or to act among the minority. But I urge you, sons and daughters of Issachar, to develop *discernment* and *direction*—to see our world clearly . . . then to play your part by doing what ought to be done.

Three Troubling Changes

Over the course of my lifetime, I have witnessed three troubling changes in our world. For those of us seeking to understand our times, it's imperative that we recognize these changes. We must discern the impact they are having so that we might offer a thoughtful and loving response.[3]

First, *I see a blurring of the line between right and wrong.* This same line also separates truth from error, so we find ourselves in a day when many refuse to call *anything* wrong. A significant shift has taken place over the last two generations. When I was growing up, my parents made clear the line between right and wrong. Everyone knew the difference. Moreover, everyone understood what happened when we crossed that line: consequences would follow! The pulpits of yesteryear clearly distinguished between good and evil. Many of those who served in political offices shared these same values. In my early years, even some individuals in the media openly declared what was right or wrong. Can you believe it? *Clearly*, it was different then!

I have seen a move from a wholesome standard of morality to a wholesale emphasis on tolerance. Our world has replaced common sense with political correctness. We often defend criminals more passionately than victims. We live in a day when calling virtually any-thing wrong marks you as bigoted and prejudiced. Standing against same-sex marriage labels you an intolerant homophobe and out of touch with reality. Stating that the Bible teaches what's right no longer carries the weight it once did. Identifying yourself as pro-life sets you apart as anti-women, narrow-minded, and lacking in compassion. Promoting abstinence as the best method for birth control—and as preparation for a wholesome and healthy marriage—means you just don't get it. In today's climate, holding to conservative moral stan-dards makes you look foolish. Why? Because there's a blurring of the line between right and wrong.

There's a second troubling change that's occurring these days: *I see a growing ignorance of biblical knowledge*. There was a time, even in my lifetime, when theological thinking, biblical understanding, and doctrinal truth were our guides for living. If Scripture said it, we considered it true and allowed it to guide our decisions. If the Word of God addressed it, that's where we began. If the Bible stated it, that's what we believed. Politicians as well as educators quoted frequently from the Scriptures. Prayer was a part of every classroom in my elementary school years. No one even *thought* of it as inappropri-ate. Presidents quoted from the Bible, and pastors spoke in favor of Holy Scripture, taking it literally and teaching it forcefully. Pulpits were known for strong doctrine and a commitment to biblical exposi-tion. But now? Sadly, in our times we have what the prophet Amos called, "a famine on the land, / Not a famine for bread or a thirst for water, / But rather for hearing the words of the LORD" (Amos 8:11). How tragic!

Now many churches masquerade as entertainment centers, where the leadership primarily concerns itself with making people feel good. Woodrow "Wood" Kroll, in his helpful work *Back to the Bible*, wrote, "When the church becomes an entertainment center, Bible literacy is usually an early casualty. People go away from the event with a smile on their face but a void in their life." [4]

Let's face it. You probably know less about the Bible than your grandparents knew. You likely stand less often for scriptural principles, even if you were raised according to them, than your own parents did. You may be an exception—already among the sons of Issachar—but most are not. The biblical ignorance in our land is, at times, heartbreaking.

Dr. Gary Burge, longtime professor of New Testament studies at Wheaton College, noted a deficiency in the entering students when it came to biblical knowledge:

> For the last four years, the Bible and theology department at Wheaton College in Illinois has studied the biblical and theological literacy of incoming freshmen. These students are intellectually ambitious and spiritually passionate. They represent almost every Protestant denomination and every state in the country. Most come from strong evangelical churches and possess a long history of personal devotion and Christian involvement (regular church attendance, youth groups, camps, missions, etc.). They use the Bible regularly—but curiously, few genuinely know its stories.
>
> The Bible has become a springboard for personal piety and meditation, not a book to be read. . . .

When asked to complete a test in which a series of biblical events must be placed in order, our students returned surprising results. One-third of the freshmen could not put the following in order: Abraham, the Old Testament prophets, the death of Christ, and Pentecost. Half could not sequence: Moses in Egypt, Isaac's birth, Saul's death, and Judah's exile. One-third could not identify Matthew as an apostle from a list of New Testament names. When asked to locate the biblical book supplying a given story, one-third could not find Paul's travels in Acts, half did not know that the Christmas story was in Matthew or that the Passover story was in Exodus. . . .

On my simple 25-question test, high-school youth groups averaged 50–55 percent correct. When these students were pooled, average responses to particular questions gave a more dramatic picture. Fully 80 percent could not place Moses, Adam, David, Solomon, [and] Abraham in chronological order. Only 15 percent could place in order the major events of Jesus' and Paul's lives. Only 20 percent knew to look in Acts to read the story of Paul's travels. And while 60 percent could locate the Exodus story in the Old Testament, only 33 percent could find the Sermon on the Mount in the New Testament, and 80 percent did not know how to find the Lord's Prayer.[5]

Shocking results. These are our children, the legacy we leave behind us to carry on in our churches. But what will those churches be like without women and men committed not only to proclaiming God's Word but also to imprinting it on their hearts?

You may have watched *The Tonight Show with Jay Leno* (even though you may not tell many people you have). Airing on NBC after the late news, the television show contains some amusing elements, while other parts slide into the crude behaviors of our day. One of

Leno's bits is hilarious—or at least it would be if it weren't so tragic. He takes his microphone out on the streets and asks questions to unsuspecting passersby about the Bible. The questions are not hard; in fact, they're designed to be easy. That's where the laughs come in.

In one such scene, Leno asked, "Name one of the Ten Command-ments." After a long pause, one man said, "Uh, God helps those who help themselves." Everybody laughed. Leno asked another, "Can you name one of the apostles?" Nobody could name one. So he said, "Okay, can you name the four Beatles?" Immediately, "John, Paul, George, Ringo." The crowd cheered. Leno moved on to another victim and said, "Let me ask you a few questions about the Bible." Answer: "Uh-oh. I . . . I don't know much about the Bible." Leno asked, "Well, can you tell me, according to the Bible, who was swallowed by a great fish?" Answer: "Pinocchio."

Sure, we laugh, but we can see in these answers a downward slide in biblical knowledge. It becomes even more tragic when it's true of Christians. If you lack biblical knowledge, you will not be able to survive these times with any sense of spiritual victory. You sit at the mercy of any persuasive leader who says, "Follow me. I'll line your pockets. I'll give you a job. I'll provide you with a future. Just go my way."

A third troubling change has occurred in our day: *I see an intensifying embrace of postmodernism.* We have clearly shifted from a Christian era to a post-Christian era. What used to be true about Great Britain and the rest of Europe has spread to the United States of America—the land I love, a country I have served to help protect. We live in a post-Christian swamp, and we have postmodernism to thank for it. Vaclav Havel said it well: "We live in the postmodern world where everything is possible and almost nothing is certain."[6]

Instead of interpreting life honestly, people now interpret it emotionally. Instead of the real being real, people now distort reality, allowing virtual reality to take charge. Many among the younger generation *prefer* virtual reality—because actual reality is too boring. We've shifted from objective thinking (based on instruction from the truth of Holy Scripture) to subjective, secular thinking (based squarely on humanism), where self always predominates.

Need a good description of postmodernism? Here you go:

> Postmodernism thrives on chaos and desires to destroy all moral criteria and replace it with no criteria. It seeks a world in which everything is relative, where there is no truth, and perception is reality. Since God's eternal truth has no place in such a world, with the rise of postmodernism we have witnessed a commensurate decline in biblical literacy.[7]

What makes postmodernism especially interesting is the way it has evolved. Postmodernism began in the elite atmosphere of the academic community. It soon flowed from the eggheads to virtually everyone in any position of leadership. It has spread from the halls of academia to the halls of Congress, to the halls of local public schools, and then to the halls and rooms of our private homes. We now live in a culture shot through with this way of thinking. Make no mistake about it—postmodernism is both insidious and subtle. No company will ever make a big announcement: "We are now embracing postmodernism!" It doesn't come in like that. It is subtle . . . and often undetected.

The greatest tragedy of all? The evangelical church of the twenty-first century has surrendered to it. We have begun to buy in to this way of thinking. Francis Schaeffer anticipated it twenty-five years ago, announcing "the great evangelical disaster—the failure of the evangelical world to stand for truth as truth. There is only one word for this—namely *accommodation*: the evangelical church has accommodated to the world spirit of the age."[8] Too often we have accommodated postmodernism, so now we can readily see its evidences in the church.

Ten Disturbing Realities about Postmodernism[9]

I've introduced you to the principles of postmodernism, but I need
to clarify further. Let me offer ten disturbing realities about postmodernism. None of them is attractive. None of them will make you
feel good. But all of them are significant if we hope to understand our
times, as the sons of Issachar did.

Number one: *no authority is valid.* This notion breaks down
important structures in our society—such as the family—and gives
people false impressions about roles and hierarchies in daily life.
Those who hold this position will challenge authority, asking *who are
you to tell me what to believe?* Respect for authority is nonexistent.

Number two: *no rules are valid.* This means that we should make
up our own minds about right and wrong, only obeying those things
we feel are right for us. In other words, if it feels right, do it. Beginning during the 1960s, this idea has taken on a more robust shape in
the 1980s, 1990s, and into the twenty-first century.

Number three: *style is more important than substance.* Here
we get the idea that reality consists only of image or appearance,
rather than substance. As I remember, a former U.S. president said
in an unguarded moment, "What does character have to do with
being the president?" Style and presentation trump substance in
postmodernism.

Number four: *morality is a matter of choice.* This mentality suggests
that it's all right to live however we want. I even know parents who
let a son and his girlfriend live together in the parents' house, under
the same roof, in the back bedroom. So, it's okay if they feel like they
should do it. People like this will make decisions based on their own
reasoning, excluding any outside authority or counsel.

Number five: *the cardinal virtue is tolerance.* This kind of tolerance
says we must validate everyone's beliefs. We can't be intolerant.
Perhaps the most intolerant of all individuals who ever lived was

Jesus Christ. The religious people crucified Him for it! They hated Him because He didn't tolerate their nonsense. At the same time, He was winsome. What a remarkable balance. However, balance is lost with today's excessive commitment to tolerance.

Number six: *words have no inherent meaning, so true communication is impossible.* Having made this point in a message once, I had a scientist come to see me afterward. He said, "I just want to thank you about what you said regarding words. My world is a world of words." He couldn't do his work without them! Scientists have to be able to agree on the meanings of words so that they can communicate clearly about their research. Words carry weight or they carry nothing. We are seeing the significance of words fade. Evidence is based on words. Decisions we make are based on words. Instruction to our children is based on words. If words—the building blocks of communication—have no inherent meaning, then nothing has meaning.

Number seven: *Western culture is oppressive.* That means logic is out, and mysticism is in. Democracy is out, and how a person feels about something is in. Objective truth is out, and subjective opinion is in. The postmodern person wonders *who are we in Western culture to think we have some kind of corner on what is right and best?* This mind-set says that someone else somewhere else always has another answer better than the answers we've been given.

Number eight: *the line between truth and entertainment is removed.* So guess what? Hollywood becomes as good a source of truth as the Bible. Now people who are in search of truth quote celebrities because of their fame rather than the substance of their words. Sports heroes guide us today where parents and the books of old gave us direction in the past. Our world has lost a sense of the difference between wisdom and entertainment.

Number nine: *images and fantasy interpret reality.* Look at video games that are filled with disturbing images, fantasy, and violence. Those images become reality for the kids who play them. So why should we be surprised that kids load up rifles and walk through halls of high schools pulling triggers? They watch unsavory behavior constantly in video games, not to mention hearing it in music, seeing it on television, and surfing it on the Internet. These images interpret reality for people of all ages—and increasingly so in these times.

Finally, number ten: *what people believe is right, so they can do anything to achieve a goal.* Feel wronged or oppressed? This mind-set suggests eliminating an opponent. Wipe him or her out! Terrorism makes all the sense in the world under this mind-set. When people think this way, no one can tell them what to do. Individuals that think like this can kidnap a missionary or bomb an embassy and sleep well that night. Postmodern thinkers believe it's acceptable to retaliate any way they wish if they feel wronged, because what *they* believe is right.

These ten realities mark our times in indelible ways. As followers of Christ, we must find our way through the morass of our age with the love, wisdom, and compassion of our Savior.

Surviving These Troubled Times

As I began, I wrote that we've come upon tough times. The bad news is even worse than that. Our times are going to get a lot tougher, especially for those of us who determine to swim upstream rather than float downstream. May I remind you that deception is on the loose? Unless you're aware of it, you'll be led down that primrose path. To steer clear, you're going to need two important things.

First, *you need discernment.* Sons and daughters of Issachar, let me urge you to cultivate discernment, for that is how you're going to survive our times. Discernment will keep you from being deceived, duped, and disillusioned. Discernment will tell you, "This is leading to a bad conclusion. I'm stopping that. I'm not going there. Our children aren't going to go there." Discernment will help you avoid the pitfalls of living in this world.

Second, *you need direction.* You need to know what you ought to do. Direction will give you an aim, a goal. It will provide you with something good to pursue. But direction will also force you to make hard decisions. Decide for yourself. Exhibit the courage to do the right thing in the face of opposition and discouragement.

My wife, Cynthia, and I, on a recent visit to Israel, spent a little more time than usual at the Yad Vashem Museum. If you ever go to Israel, don't miss it. The museum honors those killed in the Holocaust. It stands as a stark piece of architecture that stretches into the skies. The builders intentionally chose to paint it a drab, gray color—a deathly pallor, if you will. As you enter, you wind your way up and down long aisles where you see life-sized pictures of hollow-eyed individuals, who do not know exactly what was in front of them or where they were headed. When you get to the end of the museum, you enter the room of remembrance and see on shelves notebook after notebook after notebook after notebook filled with the names of the Jews who were killed, the names handwritten by the Nazis as if they were proud to record every one. How could it be? How could that happen? The museum even has preserved the iron sign that hung over the entrance of Dachau: "Work Makes You Free," it reads in German. But even that wasn't the most poignant thing I saw. What stood out was a statement made in one of the official documents passed around to all of those who were leading the camps: "The camp's law is that those going to their death should be deceived until the end." Deceived until the end.

Serious words . . . so much to think about. I know you care about the days we live in. You care about the days ahead that our children and grandchildren face. You wouldn't be reading if you didn't care. But it is so easy to be swept along by the waves of our times. In light of that, and in light of the deception we'll look at in chapter 2, we each must determine how to live our lives. I urge you to read fewer newspapers and periodicals and read more of your Bible instead. I urge you to become a serious student of the Scriptures. Take them seriously. Teach them to your children. Read them as couples and as singles. Let the Bible be your guide.

Adopting this habit will do amazing things, as it helps you hone discernment and develop direction in a world that has lost its way.

Chapter Two

Dealing with Deceivers
by Charles R. Swindoll

For the next few minutes, I want you to think about a time in your
life when you were deceived. For some of you, it may have been a
former marriage. The person you married proved to be someone other
than who you thought. The horror of living in the backwash of that
deception is almost more than you can bear to remember. Or maybe
you invested your funds with a particular individual who promised
to handle them carefully. Then you discovered that deception had
occurred right under your nose. Or perhaps you purchased a fake
diamond or bought a house plagued by problems that the real estate
agent failed to point out.

Whatever your situation, we *all* have experienced deception. Is
there anything worse than being taken advantage of?

As difficult as these shams are to endure, I will tell you of one
even worse: *spiritual deception.* Spiritual deceivers have the audacity
to misquote portions of the Bible, to take money for themselves in the
name of ministry, to promise healing while knowing they can't give it,
and to assure hope even though they have none. This kind of deception leaves you with the leftovers of a phony faith. How tragic is that?

Deception is alive and well in our world. As believers in Jesus Christ,
we must develop the discernment to recognize deception when we
see it. I offered some specific examples of cultural erosion and
deception in chapter 1. Now let's turn our attention to understanding
the roots of deception . . . and the proper approach to dealing with it.

Declaring a Conflict Many Would Deny

Even in the first century, spiritual deception was widespread. The apostle Paul had it on his heart when he wrote to the Christians in the cosmopolitan city of Corinth. Into the ranks of gullible believers came charlatans with the eloquence to speak and the charisma to win over the Corinthians. Some of these spiritual deceivers lived immorally, and the Corinthians thought their acceptance of these men expressed sacrificial grace. They essentially looked away from the immorality and said, "That's okay. Grace covers it all." They were blind to the damage of the spiritual deception in their midst. How tragic!

So Paul wrote them as a father would write his daughter or a mother would write her son, saying, "I am jealous for you with a godly jealousy; for I betrothed you to one husband, so that to Christ I might present you as a pure virgin" (2 Corinthians 11:2). Paul used the symbol of a marriage ceremony and applied it spiritually, encouraging the Corinthian believers to seek out purity in their devotion to Jesus.

Then came the contrast that changed the scene: "But I am afraid . . ." We rarely read of Paul being afraid of anything! But here we find in him a healthy fear. "I am afraid that, as the serpent deceived Eve by his craftiness, your minds will be led astray from the simplicity and purity of devotion to Christ" (11:3). Don't you just love Paul? Sometimes I just want to throw my arms around him and thank him for saying it so clearly and so well. The old serpent, when he slithered into the garden of Eden, didn't come with a sign saying, "I'm about to deceive you, Eve. Beware; I'm bringing something that you're going to spend the rest of your life regretting." Instead, he came saying, in effect, "You can be like God if you eat that fruit from that tree" (see Genesis 3:5). Eve listened just long enough for the serpent to lure her into his offer, and then she ate the fruit. Eve was deceived into sinning, but Adam knew what he was doing. Adam sinned willfully!

Satan has made a career of deception. The first mention of Satan in the Bible is in the garden of Eden, as he tempted Adam and Eve. The last scene of Satan is described in Revelation 20:10, where we read of a deceptive Satan being thrown into the lake of fire. Deception with humanity at the beginning . . . deception with humanity at the end. Considering Satan's long career and expertise in deception, don't think for a moment that he isn't busily making sin seem attractive and appealing. Of course he is! He knows that he must make us feel good in order for us to fall into his traps. Satan offers us so much, or so it seems. So attractive . . . but all phony.

Paul knew of Satan's deception and feared that the Corinthian believers might also be deceived. The two words "led astray" in 2 Corinthians 11:3 come from the single Greek term *phtheiro*. This verb means "to cause deterioration of the inner life." It came to mean "ruin" and later to mean "corrupt someone" by "erroneous teaching" or "misleading tactics."[1] Paul feared that the Corinthians would deteriorate in their inner life, that they would live with immorality in their midst for so long that they would eventually approve of it. He explained, "For if one comes and preaches another Jesus whom we have not preached, or you receive a different spirit which you have not received, or a different gospel which you have not accepted, you bear this beautifully" (2 Corinthians 11:4). Even though Paul chose the word "if," he left no doubt as to the real danger to the Corinthian Christians. "If" in this context indicates the presumption of truth—that some will surely come and preach "another Jesus." In fact, the spiritual deceivers were already there, preying on the church at Corinth. Their teaching sounded like Jesus's, looked like Jesus's, and had a message undeniably close to the message of Jesus. But it was deception. It wasn't the message Paul preached to these believers.

Now, some would say of the Corinthian's tolerant attitude, "What an amazing thing! How great it is that we have these multiple ways of looking at life." We call that pluralism, where any god will do, as long as we're sincere; any way to that god will work, as long as we feel good about it. It sounds so good, doesn't it? So politically correct. But it's a lie. Pluralism leads only to error. The Corinthians were willing to listen and accept the eloquent—or even the entertaining—preacher of an adulterated gospel that added human merit to divine grace. And they weren't the only ones! The conflict with pluralism and deception goes on to this very day. Remember, deception is Satan's career.

Announcing and Exposing Heresy

By the time John wrote his first epistle, forty years had passed since Paul wrote to the Corinthians. By then the conflict had worsened. Nearing the end of the first century, John saw that the church had become corrupted. Hard to believe, isn't it? It didn't even take a full century for the church to drift into the path of deception! John pulled no punches and addressed it head-on. This aged apostle, the last still living of the original twelve, decided that he had nothing to lose by declaring the truth as it was. He called a liar "liar," a wrong "wrong," an error "error," and truth "truth." I love John's writings! We never have to wonder where he stood.

"Children, it is the last hour," John wrote, "and just as you heard that antichrist is coming, even now many antichrists have appeared" (1 John 2:18). In chapter 1 of this book, we discussed that the singular form of "antichrist" in this verse refers to a literal individual who will one day come and rule with a persuasive ability. He will promise hope to the world by ending all conflict, pledging peace in the Middle East, and prompting reconciliation around the world. This individual is still to come—still future. In the meantime, there are "many antichrists," many who come as counterfeiters in the deceitful spirit of the coming Antichrist. These antichrists of today look like Christ or have a message that allegedly comes from Christ, but in reality they can offer only a counterfeit gospel. In today's "many antichrists," we find the roots of deception and heresy in our world.

Understanding an Important Difference

But before we can deal with the antichrists and the deceivers, we first have to make sure we can tell them apart from truth-tellers. So let's begin by exposing deception, which, in the church, we call *heresy*. Deceivers and heretics hate exposure. They love to operate under the radar.

For a long time I had a little red devil that sat on the shelf in my study. Oh it wasn't a *real* devil; it was a wooden caricature. It looked like what we *think* of when we picture the devil: pitchfork, red all over, tail . . . you get the picture. (My sister gave it to me, but that's another story!) When you pushed down its head, up came a sign that said, "Go to hell." But since I often have children in my study, I painted over the sign the word, "Welcome." What a typical caricature of the devil! What Satan really *means* is, "Come to hell with me!" — but he won't tell us that outright. He cloaks his motive under flattering words that make us feel good about ourselves. Today's antichrists have the same method. They love to operate under the radar, under the guise of something new and different, something attractive and fresh. Deception in the church began in the first century, but it continues in the twenty-first. Both then and now, deceivers want more than anything to deceive.

But what did the apostle John say about these deceivers? First, *there are many of them*, not just one or two (1 John 2:18). They come in all cultures, in all languages, in all colors, in all kinds of garb, and in all settings. Some come with a pulpit, some without a pulpit. Some appear on television, while some lurk behind the scenes. Some are known halfway around the world, while others dwell in obscurity. Many deceivers and heretics are out there, ready to deceive us everywhere they can.

Second, *many of them were once in the church.* How do we know? "They went out from us" (2:19). I would enjoy finding out just how many cult leaders were once a part of an evangelical church where the Bible was taught accurately. A church they now oppose! I suspect the number is more than we would imagine. These deceivers were once in the church.

Third, John taught that *the deceivers never really trusted in Christ alone.* John wrote, "They went out from us, but they were not really of us; for if they had been of us, they would have remained with us" (2:19). They never truly trusted Christ. John Calvin put it this way, "They who fall away had never been thoroughly imbued with the knowledge of Christ, but had only a light and a transient taste of it."[2] When we talk to someone about Christ and we hear, "Well, I go to such and such a church," it tells us *nothing* about their actual faith in

Jesus. When we talk to individuals about their faith and they refer to how long they have been in a church, or what their grandfather did, or that their dad is a preacher, it tells us nothing about their relationship with Christ. Each individual must know Christ personally. These deceivers do not. And they never have.

Finally, *deceivers prey on the unsuspecting*. What do I mean by "unsuspecting"? Those who lack biblical knowledge. That's why I stressed so hard in chapter 1 the importance of knowing the Bible. We must embrace biblical truth and think theologically in the midst of a world that has gone astray. Staying in God's Word strengthens our faith and bolsters our hope. We're not talking about a miserable existence under the terrible yoke of a taskmaster. Far from it! We're talking about living a life of faith, hope, and love! But if we don't know *how* to live the Christian life, we become vulnerable to deceiving darts. Deceivers knock on our doors. They dole out their literature. They promote their views—and often, they succeed! Why? Because, too often, we don't know the difference between truth and error. Deceivers prey on the gullible!

But what about genuine believers? Notice the "but" as John changes the scene from heretics to believers: "But you have an anointing from the Holy One, and you all know" (1 John 2:20). Unlike the heretics, Christians "have an anointing from the Holy One." John used the word *anointing* a couple of times, but he was the only writer in Scripture to use the Greek word *chrisma*. It's a symbolic term referring to the Holy Spirit. Why mention the Spirit here? Because the Spirit of God is also the "Spirit of truth" who has come and guides us into all truth (see John 16:13). Genuine believers have the capacity to know the truth. First John 2:20 says that believers "all know." Please observe it doesn't say we "know it all." There's a big difference! He means that we, as believers, all have knowledge. We all have the capacity to know what will hold us close to Christ, what will keep us strong in the storms of life, and what will help us discern truth from error. Genuine believers are indwelt by the Holy Spirit, and so they can understand the truth. Not so of deceivers.

Believers have potential discernment. Just like the Sons of Issachar! John said, "I have not written to you because you do not know the truth, but because you do know it, and because no lie is of the truth" (1 John 2:21). Think about it. Have you ever found yourself listening to someone speak and you think, *How could anyone believe that?* Or maybe you look at the throng gathered around the preacher or teacher and think, *Where are they coming from? Don't they realize the profound error in this teaching?* Unbelievers are spiritually blinded by Satan (see 2 Corinthians 4:4). Without the Spirit of God, they cannot discern the difference between truth and error. Believers, on the other hand, have the potential to spot heresy a mile away. How? Because the Spirit of God urges us to think, *That's nonsense!*

Explaining the Nature of Heresy

Deceivers deceive because they lack the transforming work of the Holy Spirit in their lives. Their lack of faith has a negative impact primarily on themselves. But their heretical teaching and influence can also make damaging inroads into the lives of Christian women and men everywhere. So let's take a look at the raw reality of heresy — both its root and its results.

First John 2:22 makes clear that the root error of a deceiver centers on a defective message regarding Jesus: "Who is the liar but the one who denies that Jesus is the Christ?" The spirit of antichrist has infected our times by spreading the denial of Christ (see 1 John 4:3). John tells it straight: the one in error denies Jesus as the true Messiah, the Son of God who took on human flesh in the incarnation. Incarnation simply refers to the moment when God became man — the virgin conception of Jesus Christ. Denying the incarnation leads to deception of the most significant kind. It compromises our faith because it denies the full deity of Jesus, making His sacrifice on the cross ineffective in dealing with our sin problem. Deceivers want us to leave behind such an "inconsequential" point of theology. No. We cannot. The stakes are too high. Jesus was God in human flesh — the God-man. In the person of Jesus Christ, God came to humanity in human form.

Because deceivers deny the true nature of Jesus as the God-man, they say things like, "He was a good man." Others might even say, "He was a prophet who temporarily became a member of the Godhead." I know a great Greek term for that way of thinking: *hogwash!* Christians have historically affirmed that Jesus has *always* been deity—at the creation of the world, before being born in the manger, while growing up as a baby and a young man, and as a crucified, resurrected, and ascended man. At *all times* Jesus has been coequal, coeternal, and coexistent with the Father. That's the truth.

Satan tempts us to not believe such "nonsense" by suggesting, *How could God be man and not be corrupted by having the same nature as man?* God handled that question beautifully. He preserved the purity of His Son from any sin through the virgin birth. God came upon Mary through the Holy Spirit and enabled the birth of the perfect Lamb of God without spot and without blemish. This event is critical to our faith, and deceivers will deny it. Remember, the message of the deceiver is not only defective, it is diabolical! Deception always finds its roots in the chief deceiver—Satan himself.

Most people want a relationship with God. Notice how John assumed this desire: "Whoever denies the Son does not have the Father; the one who confesses the Son has the Father also" (1 John 2:23). Human beings want to know God the Father. "God" is politically tolerated because our culture fills that term with its own meaning. But there's no gray area in the apostle John's mind: to know God, we must have a relationship with the Son of God. Sound too narrow? Perhaps—*unless it's true.* Jesus said, "I am the way, and the truth, and the life; no one comes to the Father but through Me" (John 14:6). Peter proclaimed, "And there is salvation in no one else; for there is no other name under heaven that has been given among men by which we must be saved" (Acts 4:12). The apostle Paul penned, "There is one God, and one mediator also between God and men, the man Christ Jesus" (1 Timothy 2:5). Get the picture? The entire New Testament testifies to the absolute necessity of faith in Christ alone for salvation.

Deceivers argue for a wider path to God, but God's Word is clear. By faith alone, in Christ alone, and because of grace alone. That's the truth about our salvation from sin. May I urge you not to be too diplomatic? May I challenge you to stand against political correctness when it comes to the person of Jesus? Don't get sucked in to the culture. Stay specific about what you believe so you can avoid the pitfalls set by those seeking to lead you astray.

John Stott put it like this:

> Christian theology is anchored not only to certain historical events, culminating in the saving career of Jesus, but to the authoritative apostolic witness to, and interpretation of, these events. The Christian can never weigh anchor and launch out into the deep of speculative thought. Nor can he forsake the primitive teaching of the apostles for subsequent human traditions.[3]

In other words, we hold on to not only the life of Jesus but also to the writings of the apostles. Jesus lived His life, and the life that He lived qualified Him for the sacrificial death that He died. The death that Jesus died qualifies us for the life that He lived. But we learn of His life, death, and resurrection in the Gospels and the letters of the New Testament. So our knowledge of and confession about Jesus is anchored in the apostolic witness about His life. When we take hold of Christ and His Word, we distinguish ourselves from the false teachers and heretics that float in and out of our lives.

Claiming the Safeguards against Deceivers

How can we guard against the message of our adversaries? First, *stay with the truth of Holy Scripture.* In 1 John 2:24, the apostle said, "As for you, let that abide in you which you heard from the beginning. If what you heard from the beginning abides in you, you also will abide in the Son and in the Father." Notice that John's focus changed from warning believers against deceivers to advising them on how to deal with deception. That's important. He wanted us to dwell on God's Word. For when we stay close to God's Word, we stay close to the Father and the Son as well. So abide in it. Don't be lured away from it.

I recently had a medical doctor tell me that he had a patient facing a pretty severe future. And he said to her very carefully and tactfully, "May I pray with you?" She said, "Yes, just so it isn't in the name of Christ." So I said, "What did you do?" He said, "Well, I wished her well and I didn't pray, because I only pray to God through Christ." He cared about her but not to the point of leading her astray by leaving out Christ Himself! We need to speak of Christ personally and directly. If His Word abides in us, He will abide in us. So stay with the truth of Holy Scripture.

The danger for us is real. Need an example? Popular author and television personality Wayne W. Dyer offers a different message. He introduces us to a "glowing celestial light" and wants us to "know the wonder of having your sacred self triumph over the demands of the ego self, which wants more than anything to hold you back."[4] Wait a minute! Where's Christ in that?

Erwin Lutzer, pastor of Moody Church, leads us away from Dyer's error:

> Contemporary spirituality defines God as an equal-opportunity employer, the universal source of energy, waiting to be tapped by all of us. What we believe is not important; the challenge is to understand ourselves in light of this higher power that is already within us. If we need forgiveness, we must simply grant it to ourselves; we have broken the commands of no personal God. Since there is no God to offend, there is no God whose forgiveness we must seek. *The craze is self-salvation by self-knowledge.*[5]

Watch out for error. Don't be sucked in by it. The first safeguard is always the Word of God.

The second safeguard is to *rely on the teaching of the Holy Spirit*. The apostle John said,

> This is the promise which He Himself made to us: eternal life. . . . And the testimony is this, that God has given us eternal life, and this life is in His Son. He who has the Son has the life; he who does not have the Son of God does not have the life. (1 John 2:25; 5:11–12)

When you have Christ, you have life. It's that simple.

But reading that, many may find themselves saying, "Man, that is narrow." That's exactly right! Too often we want to change or diminish God's teaching and make it more palatable to modern ears. But it doesn't work that way!

When I go to the airport and ask the desk attendant when the flight leaves, she doesn't say, "Well, how do you feel about it? If you'd like it to leave at 12:15, maybe around then, okay? Or . . . you probably have to have lunch, so how about 2:00?" It doesn't work like that! If they say it leaves at 1:27 p.m., what happens if I'm not there? "Get the next flight, buddy. You missed the flight." You're there or you miss it. Salvation is the same way: it's through Christ . . . or you miss it. As wise Solomon once wrote, "There is a way which seems right to a man, / But its end is the way of death" (Proverbs 14:12). We need to trust the teaching of the Holy Spirit, who alone offers eternal life.

> These things I have written to you concerning those who are trying to deceive you. As for you, the anointing which you received from Him abides in you, and you have no need for anyone to teach you; but as His anointing teaches you about all things, and is true and is not a lie, and just as it has taught you, you abide in Him. (1 John 2:26–27)

How great is that! Rely on what the Spirit of God teaches you. This passage isn't belittling the importance of human teachers; it's saying that believers have the capacity to grasp the truth. How? From the Word of God and the Spirit of God.

Walking in Triumph

Let's get practical. How do you walk in triumph in a world that has lost its way? Let me give you three simple statements. First, *renew your commitment to the Word of God*. Don't let the sun set on any day without spending some time on your own reading the Scriptures. Think of it as filling your tank with gas so that you can run your course without running dry. God's Word will give you direction for the decisions you make. You'll find hope in its promises and historical accounts. And it will become more eloquent to you than anything else you hear or read.

Second, *stand firm in your convictions*. When you stand firm, believe me, you will stand out in most groups. Be ready to give an answer, and don't be shy about it. Be gracious and bold. Speak your mind. Tell the truth. Stand up and be heard.

I think one of Charles Colson's best books is *A Dance with Deception*, in which he wrote,

> Vast numbers of Americans accept certain New Age beliefs and practices.
>
> About half believe in extrasensory perception. More than a third believe in mental telepathy. A quarter of all Americans believe in astrology. A quarter believe in reincarnation. And a fifth say they've been in touch with the dead.
>
> What a testimony to the sorry state of America's spiritual condition. People are starving spiritually, yet what they're picking up to eat is the spiritual equivalent of a Twinkie. They're filling up on spiritual junk food—when what they really need is the plain but nourishing bread of the gospel.[6]

Colson has seen the myriad dangers in our world. We need to stand up in the face of error and deception. Hold on to your convictions. Stand firm!

Third, *stay focused on Christ.* Think of your focus as a laser beam. Let your mind, like a laser, point to Christ. Make Christ your specialty. Examine His life. Emulate His methods. Rest in Him. Think about Him daily. Ask yourself, *What would my Savior do if He were right here in this circumstance?*

Recently, Cynthia and I had to visit with a physician regarding a thyroid difficulty she was facing—they wanted to examine a nodule. Cynthia had researched all the possible doctors in the area and found an individual who is not only an endocrinologist but a *specialist* in the thyroid. His whole practice revolves around the thyroid. As he was getting ready to do the procedure, I decided to ask him some questions.

"You work with the thyroid?"

He said, "I do."

"What else do you do?"

"Nothing."

"You teach on the thyroid?"

"I do teach on the thyroid," he said.

"Really? You do research?"

"Yes . . . on the thyroid."

"How about other . . .?"

"No."

"Well, do you do surgery?"

"No. I do *thyroids.*" Then he looked at me and asked, "Kind of weird, isn't it?"

"As a matter of fact, no," I answered. "I love it! I wish you majored in nodules on thyroids."

He smiled, "I do."

So when he called us after the exam and said, "Everything's great. No problem," do you know what I thought? I didn't even question it. Why? Because he only does thyroids! Why do I like that? Because when someone I love has a problem with her thyroid, I want a reliable opinion on how that thyroid is doing.

In the same way, you need to major on Christ. Jesus Christ needs to be your specialty. He's our Master. He's our Lord. He's our Savior. There's none other. There's no other way to know God apart from Christ. Thinking like that simplifies our lives. It helps us place our focus where it needs to be. So when the culture offers forty-five different wrong-headed answers outside of Jesus, we can offer a reliable answer with substance. Isn't that great?

Deception is everywhere, and now is the time to think straight. We must discern the chasm between truth and error. Now is the time to prepare ourselves with the only answer that brings true and lasting satisfaction—our Lord and Savior Jesus Christ.

$\mathcal{F}$ear and Love

A Healthy Balance

Chapter Three

Fear and Love
A Healthy Balance
by Joe Harms

THE HEART OF THE MATTER

While jogging in my neighborhood recently, I came around a corner to see two middle school-aged boys walking on the sidewalk toward me, about a block away. I noticed they were walking side-by-side, and I thought to myself, "I wonder if they'll drop into single file to let me pass, or if both of them will step aside on the grass."

As the distance between us closed, I moved to the far right of the sidewalk to give the nonverbal signal that I would be using that side of the walk. I noticed no movement from the boys at all. When I was about ten feet from a collision, I realized they were not going to budge . . . in fact, they actually spread out a bit, as if to show they were not going to give an inch to the gray-haired man jogging toward them.

I took a quick detour onto the grass to avoid hitting them and muttered to myself in surprise, "Times have changed!" And then my old sin nature imagined the entire scene again, but this time I lowered my shoulder into them and said, "Excuse me!" as they tumbled onto the grass . . . but that scene wouldn't fit Christ's teachings from the Sermon on the Mount, would it (Matthew 5:38–39)?

Times *have* changed. This isolated incident is just one example of the growing trend in our culture—our youth do not have the same respect for their elders that past generations possessed. And when confronted with any kind of authority, they either challenge it or openly defy it.

And we shouldn't be surprised. As Chuck Swindoll reminded us in chapter 1, "Jesus Himself . . . predicted such times as these" (page 1). And Paul warned us that "there will be terrible times in the last days" (2 Timothy 3:1 NIV).

Look closely at 2 Timothy 3:1–5 and list the phrases that seem to characterize many young people today.

_____

_____

_____

_____

_____

Why do you think these attitudes and actions are so prevalent?

_____

_____

_____

_____

 DISCOVERING THE WAY
While the Bible does warn us that terrible times are coming, should we as Christian parents throw up our hands and resign ourselves to the inevitable? Of course not! I have been encouraged to see many parents doing an excellent job of training their preteens to obey authority and show respect to others . . . even in the midst of this current culture.

In this chapter, we'll look at three key elements I believe are necessary in order for preteens to grasp this concept; namely, that a proper attitude toward authority must be _taught_, _modeled_, and _enforced_ by parents.

Teaching a Proper Attitude toward Authority

In order to have a biblical worldview, a child must understand the basic concept of the sovereignty of God. From early childhood, he or she needs to hear about the Creator of the universe, our almighty, all-knowing, and eternal Lord God. Our children need to hear us talking about Him as the source of all things and the One to whom we owe our very existence. Without this basic understanding, it is easy to fall into the "self-esteem" deception that is so prevalent today, often promoting the concept that the child is the center of the universe!

This omnipotent, omniscient, and eternal King has asked us to both love Him and fear Him. The balance between those two points is crucial. If we overemphasize one or the other in the training of our children, we will negatively impact their concept of God.

My sense is that Christian parents today do a good job of teaching about God's love. We know the simple message of John 3:16 that echoes throughout the Bible: God loves us and wants to have a personal relationship with us. We enjoy teaching our children about the beautiful scene in which Christ said, "Let the little children come to me" (Matthew 19:14 NIV). And we teach them to be grateful that the curtain that separated humanity from God's presence was torn when Christ died for our sins, so we can now have "confidence to enter the holy place by the blood of Jesus" (Hebrews 10:19). And I often hear parents and Sunday school teachers emphasizing those three powerful words written by the apostle John: "God is love" (1 John 4:8).

However, I am concerned that we are concentrating all our efforts on teaching this one attribute of God, and we are somewhat lacking in teaching a proper fear and respect for Him.

As a quick refresher on what the Bible teaches regarding a proper fear of the Lord and obedience to His commands, summarize the following passages in your own words.

Psalm 33:8

_____

_____

_____

Leviticus 26:14–39

_____

_____

_____

Proverbs 9:10

_____

_____

_____

Proverbs 19:23

_____

_____

_____

Luke 12:5

_____

_____

_____

1 John 5:3

_____

_____

_____

   Your children will face many fears during their preteen years. "Will I ever look normal?" "Will I be popular?" "Will I have a good career, a good family?" All of these fears are reduced greatly, and may even vanish, if you can help your son or daughter learn to fear the Lord and trust Him with their lives.

Think back on occasions in the Bible when God revealed Himself in one way or another to a human. What was the person's normal, appropriate reaction when he or she reflected on the majesty of God? Describe the reactions of the following three men:

Job (31:23; 40:4)

_____

_____

_____

Isaiah (6:1–13)

_____

_____

_____

Peter (Luke 5:8)

_____

_____

_____

As we reflect on how these men responded to being in God's presence, what applications can we draw from our own relationship with God and how we approach Him in our prayer lives? Because, as believers, we have the Holy Spirit already living within us, should we even be concerned with how we approach God? After all, He wants us to "pray without ceasing" (1 Thessalonians 5:17), so why can't we just think of Him as our good buddy?

When we teach about prayer in our preteen ministry, the senior pastor and I enjoy putting on a short skit for the kids. At some point during the lesson, Pastor Chuck pops in and states that he "just wants to spend some time hanging out with the preteens." Instead of greeting him with respect or welcoming him to our class, I immediately begin to steer him around the room, asking for various things . . . "We need more space," "We need a larger budget," and "Will you see that we get another foosball table in here?"

During the skit, the preteens sit in shock, wondering to themselves, *Why is Pastor Joe being so impolite and disrespectful?*

After I rudely dismiss our senior pastor and guide him out the door without a single kind word or even a "thank you," the room explodes with righteous indignation!

"Why did you treat him like that?!"

"That was mean, Pastor Joe!"

My personal favorite is, "Don't you realize that's your boss? You could lose your job!"

And then I ask them, "How was that conversation I just had with Pastor Chuck like our own prayer life with God?" And they get it! They come up with all the key points: we usually don't take time to listen to God; we tend to just concentrate on our requests, instead of praising Him and thanking Him; and we don't approach Him with the respect and honor He deserves. Our conclusion is this: if we need to treat our senior pastor with respect and honor, how much more should we display these attitudes when we spend time with the Creator of the universe?

I was thrilled to hear one of our moms tell me later that her son's prayer life had changed, that he was careful to spend time praising God and naming some of His attributes in worship before making any personal requests. This young man is well on his way to gaining a healthy fear of the Lord.

Modeling a Proper Attitude toward Authority

We can teach sound, biblical doctrine regarding obedience to God and to the authorities He has placed in our lives, but if we are not living it out day-by-day, our words ring hollow. We all know that children learn far more from watching us than listening to us. Truth that is "caught" reaches far deeper than truth that is "taught."

For this reason, I would recommend you complete this part of the Bible study together with your preteen son or daughter and discuss various ways that you personally submit to authorities that God has ordained. Your personal examples will speak volumes.

Complete the sentences below by filling in the missing words.

Ephesians 6:5 (NIV): Slaves, _____ your _____ _____ with _____ and _____ . . . just as you would _____ _____.

Colossians 3:20 (NIV): Children, _____ your _____ in _____, for this pleases _____ _____.

Hebrews 13:17 (NIV): _____ your leaders and _____ to their authority. They keep watch over you as men who must give an _____. Obey them so that their work will be a _____, not a _____, for that would be of no advantage to you.

According to Ephesians 6:1–9 and Paul's parallel passage in Colossians 3:18–25, whose authority are we really following when we obey "parents" or "earthly masters"?

_____

_____

Thankfully, we do not have "slaves and masters" in most of the world today, but we do have other situations where this truth would apply. Together with your preteen children, make a list of all the authorities God has placed in your lives.

_____   _____

_____   _____

_____   _____

_____   _____

_____   _____

_____   _____

As a parent, think of two or three situations where you chose to submit to authority, even though you disagreed with the person giving the orders or making the rules. Take some time to discuss these situations with your preteen.

Situation	Rule or command you were told to obey
_____	_____
_____	_____
_____	_____

Conclude your time with prayer, asking God to provide strength and courage to obey in the tough situations that you and your preteen will encounter through the course of a typical day.

I thought I understood what it meant to "respect your elders" and "obey all authorities" until I lived in Thailand. I had the privilege of serving at an international Christian school in Bangkok for nine years, and I'll never forget the culture shock of that first year. Some of my Thai students would approach my desk at a crouch, then drop to a kneeling position and offer their homework to me almost like a sacrifice — lifted up and held high above their bowed heads. It took months to convince them that they could stand straight when they approached their teachers. Most Asian cultures do an excellent job of teaching children to respect their elders, and teachers are held in especially high regard. In a typical Asian society, it is simply unthinkable to argue with a teacher or question his or her authority.

It saddens me to think that in America, which was once a Christian nation and is still labeled as "Christian" by most of the world, our youth do not compare favorably with a Buddhist nation like Thailand when it comes to obeying authority.

Thankfully, that does not have to be the case in your own home. As we will discuss in the next section, you have the responsibility and the opportunity to set your own standards for your children and to teach them this crucial concept of obedience to God and to the authorities He has ordained.

Enforcing a Proper Attitude toward Authority

A friend told me jokingly that if outer-space aliens could see all the humans following their little pet dogs around their neighborhoods, picking up their droppings that they carefully save in plastic bags, they might well assume that dogs rule Earth!

As ridiculous as that sounds, some of my observations of parents and their preteens make me wonder who is in charge of their homes.

For example, a mom will come to pick up "Johnny" after our ministry event has concluded for the evening. She is already weary from a full day of work. I watch her follow Johnny around the room, picking up his forgotten Bible and papers and pleading with him gently, "We need to go now . . . Mommy's tired . . . please, Johnny . . . it's time to leave."

I tend to remain quiet in these situations, silently repeating to myself, "You're the pastor, not the parent." But then Johnny yells to his mom, "Hang on a sec! I'm going to play one more game of air hockey!"—and I can't hold back any longer. While I'm unplugging the air hockey game, I tell Johnny, "Your mother said it was time to go home."

A large part of the problem lies with the fact that we have created a society in America where parents feel uncomfortable disciplining their children in public. And when it comes to other people's children? Hands off! As Leslie Pepper writes, "These days it's just not PC to police other people's children." [1]

The church community can and should be different from the "politically correct" culture that surrounds us. As parents, we can discuss our discipline standards with the parents of our preteen's friends and work together to maintain basic rules of behavior in our various homes. For example, if your daughter is going to a friend's house for a sleepover, you could review a few basic rules with the other child's parent beforehand and let your preteen know. "Becky, remember Mrs. Linda will expect you to obey the first time she asks you to do something" and "Mrs. Linda has permission to call me if you are giving her any trouble, and I'll come pick you up immediately."

One of the scariest principles I've ever heard is this: my children's concept of *God the Father* is largely influenced by how I interact with them as their *earthly father*.

Do you agree with that statement? And if so, how should that affect your parenting? (Although it primarily applies to dads, moms can answer this question also.)

_____

_____

_____

_____

_____

STARTING YOUR JOURNEY
Please accept some friendly advice from a former middle school/high school principal. As parents, don't make the same mistake I saw a number of rookie teachers make: whether consciously or unconsciously, their number-one priority often became, "Get the kids to like me." These first-year teachers bent over backward to be "cool" and "entertaining," and often they did succeed in becoming very popular among the student body. However, in the process they made many compromises in both student classroom behavior and academic achievement. Often, I overheard the same students who appeared to adore those teachers talk about them by their lockers, saying things like, "He's so easy" or "We don't get anything done in that class." Clearly, promoting an imbalanced approach to authority was ineffective and even detrimental.

We have looked at Scriptures that tell us clearly that God desires for us to both love Him and to fear Him. Would it logically follow, then, that if we desire to be godly parents—parents who display the character and qualities of God—that we would also seek for our children to love us and fear us?

For a brief self-evaluation, place an "X" on the line below to represent where you are as a parent as you try to maintain a proper balance regarding "love" and "fear."

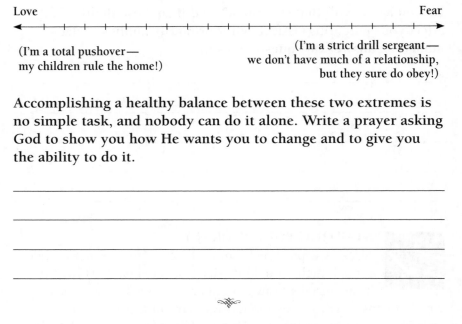

Love   Fear

(I'm a total pushover — my children rule the home!)

(I'm a strict drill sergeant — we don't have much of a relationship, but they sure do obey!)

Accomplishing a healthy balance between these two extremes is no simple task, and nobody can do it alone. Write a prayer asking God to show you how He wants you to change and to give you the ability to do it.

_____

_____

_____

_____

Your God-given assignment is to parent your children. So be the parent. Don't be their "buddy." They have plenty of buddies at school. What they need is a parent. The "friendship" and "mutual respect" will hopefully come in time, but right now in their preteen years they need a firm, consistent, and loving authority to set the standards and provide the boundaries.

Of course, they will become angry with you at times, and I doubt they will thank you for taking the time to enforce your standards. I can't remember any of my three children making this comment at the dinner table: "Father, thank you so much for grounding me this weekend. You have really helped me to gain a healthy respect for authority. I will be eternally grateful for this life lesson you have instilled within me."

Whether they are old enough to understand the reasons or not, our preteens need someone to teach, model, and enforce a healthy fear of God and a respect for the authorities God has placed in their lives. I like the simplicity of the phrase my friend's dad used to tell him when he was a preteen—"Son, when your mom's right, she's right. And when she's wrong . . . she's right." What a crucial concept! Children need to learn to obey their parents at an early age—whether they agree with them or not.

Parents, if you love your children—and I'm sure you do—then teach them to fear God and respect the authorities He has placed in their lives. A healthy fear of the Lord will provide a proper perspective for everything else in life. As Lloyd John Ogilvie, former chaplain to the United States Senate, said:

> There's a disturbing loss of awe and wonder in our contemporary understanding of our relationship with God. We've dropped the bracing biblical phrase "the fear of the Lord" from our list of Christian virtues. That's frightening. Literally. Terror grips us when we lose our fear of God. Without that one creative fear, we have no defense against all our destructive fears.[2]

Transitions

Navigating the Waters of Middle School

Chapter Four

Transitions
Navigating the Waters of Middle School
by David Ake

 THE HEART OF THE MATTER
Ray Johnston, in his classic work *Developing Spiritual Growth in Junior High Students*, shared the story of a father who, along with his wife, raised several self-reliant, responsible, and God-honoring teenagers. When asked how he had done it, he mentioned a specific family tradition that took place every time one of their children reached the eighth grade.

> At the start of their last year of junior high school, each of his kids was given all of the responsibility for handling the family finances. They paid the bills, cashed the checks, handled the investments, the whole banana. He could tell that I was shocked. He said, "Kids are much more capable than we think. They just need someone in their life that believes that." [1]

That final statement is the perfect intersection of the incredible opportunity and challenge that lies before you as parents of junior high students. We dream of seeing our own junior high kids be responsible, intelligent, wise, godly, respectful, and capable.

Chuck Swindoll offered some sobering, profound, and insightful thoughts in the first two chapters of this book. He also pointed out that an undeterred and unstoppable current of hope remains in our troubled times: guided by the truth of God's Word, those who follow God vigilantly (especially parents) are uniquely "salt and light" in our world today. This lesson discusses some practical ways you can continue the process of growth in which you so heavily invested when you cradled your newborn in your arms. Also, this lesson will challenge you to consider and believe in the incredible opportunity you have before you to see your junior high student continue his or her journey to become a man or woman of Issachar fame! So let's get started.

 DISCOVERING THE WAY
At a summer camp for junior high students I attended a few years ago, the wise leader highlighted two things as we prepared for the week and looked around the grounds. First, he emphasized landmarks—grand, majestic points of interest that stood out above the horizon. He mentioned that if we were lost at any time, we could always figure out where we were in the camp by looking at those landmarks. Second, he gave a clear admonition to look out for warning signs. These were not just boundaries to respect but a "situational awareness" that one had to have to enjoy the camp. Warning signs showed us things that we either needed to avoid altogether or to handle carefully. We can see both landmarks and warning signs in the lives of junior high students as well.

Landmarks

As we travel through the landscape of early adolescence or the junior high/middle school years, we need to look for some specific signs that will help us know where we are on the journey and what may be happening when we are around these landmarks.

Landmark One: junior high students are in a time of transition. In the early adolescent years, some of the most radical developmental changes occur in a person's life. With the exception of one or maybe two of the following areas, your junior high student will experience these changes:

- Physical: growing from a child's body to an adult's body.

- Spiritual: changing from believing the faith of their family to making their own spiritual journey.

- Family: moving from having everything done for them to being a contributor in more significant ways.

- Educational: moving from simply learning to achieving.

- Social: moving from "playing well with others" to choosing and nurturing relationships on their own.

- Personal: moving from the basic simplicity of childhood to the complex, intellectual, and emotional world of adulthood.

- Financial: moving from piecemeal to manager.

Though each of these processes takes years to develop, when they are all combined together and coupled with the other landmarks we'll see later, massive change takes place in the momentum and consistency of these areas in the life of a junior high student.

Take a few minutes to discuss and reflect with your spouse or another significant adult in the life of your junior high student what changes you anticipate or have observed already in these seven areas. List them here.

_____

_____

_____

_____

How has your junior high student reacted or dealt with these changes?

_____

_____

_____

_____

Is the process of change going roughly or smoothly for him or her? Explain your answer.

_____

_____

_____

_____

Landmark Two: junior high students are expanding their capabilities. This is especially apparent in their physical and intellectual development. The physical dimensions are quite obvious: the changes in their hair, height, voice, and other characteristics go into overdrive, and they are stronger and able to run farther and faster than before. Just as significant but sometimes a bit harder to catch is the intellectual shift. Junior high students transition from concrete thinkers to abstract reasoners. The black and white of their early years become a thousand shades of gray. They now question and deconstruct the solid truths of childhood in an effort to find out how these truths work.

Landmark Three: junior high students are mature (for their age). Okay, after you stop laughing, understand that junior high students are mature in that they can accomplish much with what they have available. Roberta Hestenes was asked, "What exactly is spiritual maturity? What does it look like?" She explained it this way:

> Maturity is engaging in behavior that is appropriate
> to the stage in which you are. A 4-year-old is mature
> when he or she does everything it's reasonable for
> a 4-year-old to do. We don't consider a 4-year-old
> immature because he can't do what a 12-year-old
> does. But if he doesn't do the things 4-year-olds are
> capable of, then he's immature. So one definition of
> maturity is living up to the capacities God has made
> possible for you.[2]

Junior high students can carry out responsible adult behavior (such as proper manners) to the point that they are *equipped* and *able* to do so. During their junior high years, they rapidly gain these abilities and skill levels. However, it is important to remember that they do not all occur at once.

Landmark Four: junior high students are engaged in discovery (which makes them consistently inconsistent). Isn't it great to have at least one thing consistent during these years? As different abilities and skills show up, junior high students are eager to try them. Consequently, they are capable of responsible behavior, but they won't necessarily be consistently responsible all the time.

As loving parents, these landmarks are points in your child's journey into adulthood during which you can provide comfort, encouragement, and navigation points for the road ahead.

Warning Signs

As you guide your junior high students through their growing process and prepare them for their entry into the world, here are some warning signs about the culture to keep in mind. These warning signs are not present to make us abandon the culture but to navigate it wisely.

Warning Sign One: recognize that everything in culture has its own agenda. Just as in nature, nothing is benign, so in our modern culture, everything has an angle. Through the power of influence (and some slick marketing), culture finds ways to get people (especially junior high students) to help it survive.

Warning Sign Two: the culture sees junior high students as consumers. While many different groups claim to value junior high students, culture values them because of the potentially $190 billion-a-year purchasing power of the junior high and high school market.[3] With this much money being spent, someone is definitely looking to cash in on the opportunity.

Warning Sign Three: the culture studies junior high students and markets to them accordingly. By searching out budding cultural ideas, the culture tries to make money by mass marketing and selling these ideas to junior high students and other teens. It creates what Douglas Rushkoff calls the "feedback loop" of teen marketing. Junior high students find something that is fun, new, and "cool." The marketing culture identifies this, and all of a sudden *everybody's* doing this and buying it! It then runs its course, and the teens move on to find the next thing that suits their fancy . . . all under the watchful eyes of the culture.[4]

Warning Sign Four: nothing is sacred in pursuing this agenda. Much like the Aesop's fable of "The Goose That Laid the Golden Eggs," the culture is bent on greedily devouring its source of wealth. It constantly pushes the envelope in the discovery of the newest and greatest thing for teens. As Chuck Swindoll pointed out in chapter 1, our culture embraces the death of absolutes, words lose their meanings, and values are relative.

Is our culture the single culprit responsible for where we are today? Are we then to abandon culture and run for the hills? Absolutely not. A fallen world, a lost humanity, and the cultural revolutions of the last fifty years all form a brilliantly complex path to our condition today. Just as the sons of Issachar "understood the times," we must realize that these are landmarks and warning signs that will help us as we navigate rather than escape the culture in which we find ourselves.

How savvy is your junior high student to marketing? Explain your answer.

_____

_____

_____

_____

How can someone become a student of culture without being overly influenced by it?

_____

_____

_____

_____

What are some reliable sources that you can refer to for help in understanding current trends in culture?

_____

_____

_____

_____

STARTING YOUR JOURNEY

With our landmarks established and our warning signs recognized, how do we equip, disciple, and prepare our junior high followers of Christ not just to navigate but to engage the culture they live in? The impetus is certainly present in the passage Chuck mentioned in chapter 1: "The sons of Issachar [were] men who understood the times, with knowledge of what Israel should do" (1 Chronicles 12:32). Chuck also shared ten realities of postmodernism. In our fast-paced world, junior high students face every one of these realities multiple times a day. Instead of trying to address each one, consider a few comprehensive, practical steps or skills that you can pass along to your junior high child to help him or her meet the challenges of the culture.

Practical Step One: make sure your junior high child knows the absolutes.

Webster's defines *absolute* as

> free from imperfection . . . pure . . . having no restriction, exception, or qualification . . . positive, unquestionable . . . independent of arbitrary standards of measurement . . . fundamental, ultimate . . . perfectly embodying the nature of a thing . . . being self-sufficient and free of external references or relationships.[5]

Let's see if we find a parallel here. What is something absolute that we could recognize and relate to that is perfect, pure, unrestricted in any way (omnipotent); unquestionable and independent of any standard of measurement (omniscient and sovereign); and in perfect harmony and relationship with itself (self-sufficient, existing eternally, and in a perfect triune relationship)?

These are some of the most important characteristics of our sovereign God! Now it would certainly be an easy answer to say that if junior high students know about God they can deal with postmodernism, but that answer is a bit too simplistic. An important relationship must be established here. If God is absolute in Himself, then things that proceed from Him will be absolute as well. Consider these: absolute authority, absolute truth, and absolute morality. All three of these things and more are found in the person, character, and work of God. God has also chosen not to keep these things a secret; He has revealed His person, work, and character not only through His creation (Romans 1:18–20) but also through His revealed Word.

So when postmodernism challenges our junior high students by declaring that no authority is valid and that no rules are valid, we can point out that God has established order, intent, and design and that harmony follows the obedience to God's moral law.

How can you teach your junior high child absolutes? Consider these two practical goals: first, teach him or her the narrative of God's story in Scripture. Second, make it a goal to walk him or her through solid theology. While we can know the story of Scripture, the truths and doctrine of Scripture are just as significant. From these, the cohesive defense of God's moral absoluteness can begin.

Practical Step Two: make sure your junior high student can read well. How does a student read well? He or she does so by reading:

- *Widely*—When students read widely, they wrestle with a variety of ideas which allows them to strengthen their own identity as Christians.

- *Deeply*—Does your student know how to read beyond the surface level? Can he or she understand a book's message, recognize how it stands up to Scripture, and discern how to apply it?

- *Reflectively*—Does he or she know how to separate the "wheat" from the "chaff" in the literature, to know what to adopt and what to reject?

As Chuck mentioned, postmodernism has eroded the meaning of words as well as blurred the lines between reality and fantasy. Teaching your junior high student to read widely, deeply, and reflectively will help your student confront the postmodern subtleties in the knowledge he or she is exposed to.

Practical Step Three: teach your junior high student to find and value wisdom. The Bible Knowledge Commentary notes that "in the Bible's Wisdom literature being wise means being skilled in godly living. Having God's wisdom means having the ability to cope with life in a God-honoring way." [6] The book of Proverbs is a treasure chest of practical wisdom in Scripture, exhorting God's people to fully embrace wisdom (Proverbs 1:2). If you would like your junior high student to be able to deal with postmodernism, master the book of Proverbs with him or her!

Wisdom is the synthesis of knowing the absolutes of God's person and work and mastering the learned art of reading. God calls us to skillful living, not just shrewd living or street smarts but the type of rare skill one only finds in the most talented and dedicated craftsperson. As you seek to put the wisdom of Proverbs into practice with your student, consider these three ideas:

- Encourage your student to read from Proverbs daily, categorizing individual proverbs by the character quality each addresses.

- Spend time discussing regularly the lessons you and your student can glean from Proverbs.

- Help your student to apply the wisdom of Proverbs to his or her everyday circumstances.

Take a moment to review the practical steps listed above. In which area do you sense your junior high student has the greatest need? What can you do to guide him or her in that area?

_____

_____

_____

Steps for the Journey

Just as the sons of Issachar in 1 Chronicles "understood the times," we have looked at some specifics about junior high students and the way culture treats them today. Let me offer you a few final tips for the journey with your child through early adolescence.

First, *take a moment to remember and relish the fact that God Himself ordained you as the parent, mentor, teacher, and guide for your junior high student.* God has handed you command of this army of one, two, or however many children are in your family. Even though both the culture and your child will change, you will always be the parent!

Second, *remember that your relationship with your young teenager is in a transitional state as well.* You have been acting as a fence, closely watching and directing your child within clear and narrow boundaries. But as he or she grows older, you function as more of a lighthouse, guiding your increasingly independent child toward the safe harbors of life.

During this lighthouse stage, the goal is not independence for your child. Instead, aim for interdependence. Imagine that the life of your teenager is a grand ship being built day by day, piece by piece. When your child is finally ready, he or she will take short trips near shore and, eventually, will sail completely out of the harbor into the open sea. Lighthouses and ships depend on one another. The ship is free to move off and sail as close or as far away as it will. However, whenever the ship comes close to land, it needs a beacon, a fixed source of light that will both illuminate danger and signal the way to safety and harbor. So it is with interdependency: you build a lifelong relationship with your sons and daughters that will not end when they become functionally independent (or financially independent, for that matter). As parents, the trick comes in our having the wisdom to know when to move from being a "fence" to a "lighthouse" in the different areas of our teenagers' lives.

Third, *remember to major on the majors and minor on the minors.* In other words, use wisdom to discern big lessons and principles that are immutable in the development of your junior high student.

Finally, *young teenagers best learn to live life through deep, consistent personal relationships and appropriate experiences.* While MTV pays millions of dollars to figure that out, you already have all the tools and opportunities in your home.

In what ways are you a "fence" to your junior high student? In what ways are you a "lighthouse"?

_____

_____

_____

By arming your sons and daughters with the absolute truths of Scripture, empowering them to learn (through reading), and helping them value wisdom and discover it on their own, you will be investing significantly in pointing them in the right direction so they can navigate the waters of our culture and someday be lighthouses of their own.

$\mathcal{F}$earless Parenting

Preparing Your High School Student for a World Gone Mad

'Hear, O Israel! The LORD is our God, the LORD is one! You shall love the LORD your God with all your heart and with all your soul and with all your might. These words, which I am commanding you today, shall be on your heart. You shall teach them diligently to your sons and shall talk of them when you sit in your house and when you walk by the way and when you lie down and when you rise up."

Chapter Five

Fearless Parenting
Preparing Your High School Student for a World Gone Mad
by Jason Stevenson

THE HEART OF THE MATTER

Almost every conscientious parent I know has lost sleep contemplating his or her child's teenage years and wondering, *How are we going to survive these years?* The prospect of a Christian teenager rebelling and following the world's ways fills parents' (and often ministry leaders') hearts with worry, fear, and panic.

Adding to our fears is the truth that our culture embraces all manner of evil and calls it good. The culture's primary obstacle, the Bible, is under savage assault, labeled irrelevant and cast aside. With God's Word out of the way, the cultural environment becomes ripe for a philosophy based upon a rejection of transcendent authority and objectivity—postmodernism.

Even though these troubled times can drive us to panic, God is working out His divine plan, one in which you, as Christian parents of high school students, play an intricate part. In addition to His ever present help, God has given us His Word from which we can build a worldview—a way of looking at reality—that directly contradicts the worldview embraced by our culture. This biblical worldview affirms the transcendent authority of our Creator and His objective standard of what is right and good (Matthew 28:18; Revelation 22:13).

In my view, the task of Christian parents is to help children see the world as God intended it, with Him at its center and His people in submission to His authority. You are also to help point out the folly of following after a philosophy of life that is lived by subjective whim.

57

How, then, can you accomplish this, especially when your high school students are just about to leave home and make lives of their own?

 DISCOVERING THE WAY
Parenting children during their high school years means facing the reality that as they become adults you must hand over the stewardship of their lives to them. I have created a "mission" statement for what I believe parents and ministry leaders should be trying to accomplish at the final hands-on stage: *We are preparing our children to meet the world in all of its sinfulness by preparing them to make godly choices.*

Have you considered that releasing your child is only a few years away? How are you and your spouse going to prepare for this event or mark it as a special rite of passage for your son or daughter?

_____

_____

_____

_____

_____

What decision do you foresee your high school child making in the next five to ten years that you would like to have a conversation with him or her about?

_____

_____

_____

_____

_____

What are some of the realities of the world to which your high school child needs to be alerted?

_____

_____

_____

_____

_____

Casting a Vision and Executing a Plan

Parents of high school students should create a vision, a plan, for the remaining time they have with their children before they leave the home. What would you like to accomplish in order to prepare your children for their adult life? Have you created an environment that enables your plan to succeed? Let's take a look at three ideas that will help you answer these questions.

Define the Battles You Will Fight

During adolescence, the exercise of independent decision making and self-expression is a natural process of development to help students prepare for adulthood. Parents often see this increasing struggle for independence as a power play and usurpation of their authority. However, wise parents see the need to help their children become more independent. The secret is to tie their freedom to clear responsibilities and obligations, along with corresponding consequences for failure to meet those responsibilities and obligations.

I remember the day my mother permitted me to get a styled haircut. For about six months I had the hardest, spikiest hair in my freshman class. My mom, in her wisdom, allowed me the opportunity to express myself in a harmless way. I continued to experiment with different hairstyles until I became bald! It may seem like a minor issue, but I look back with fondness that my mom gave me the freedom to make a choice. It felt like a gift.

Hairstyles are probably the types of issues that aren't worth fighting over. Reserve your authoritative muscle for moral, spiritual, and legal obligations. These are the nonnegotiables.

For example, it is my personal conviction that parents should not allow a teenager self-expression when it comes to the child attending or not attending church. Nor do I believe is it wise to allow children to attend a church separate from the rest of the family. Regular church attendance by the entire family is an important obligation to the unity of both your immediate family and the church family (see Hebrews 10:25). Your high school teenagers' contentment at church lies in helping them make deep, abiding relationships with other adults and peers who can help them mature in their relationship with Christ.

Teenagers should also be required to spend time with the family in the home, which will not only strengthen family bonds but will help them make moral choices when outside the home. Time spent at home can be time spent in explaining to teenagers the dangers of alcohol and drugs, or the Bible's perspective on sex outside marriage, or the ethics of cheating at school.

Additionally, every teenager needs a list of clearly defined respon-sibilities, which may include a curfew, communication requirements, home chores, and parameters in using a vehicle. Teenagers should also know the logical reasons why the obligations exist. God, too, often reveals the "whys" behind His commands; they are carefully thought out and executed. For example, the mandate against sexual activity outside of marriage is supported by a litany of reasons why, both biblical and logical. The same "why" should accompany the obligations we place on our teenagers, because it teaches them that authority is not based on whim but on logical, objective reasoning and the Word of God. With these responsibilities, parents should state clearly defined consequences for failing to meet expectations. As the child matures, parents should develop a list of expected freedoms, new responsibilities, and adjustments to current obligations. For example, a curfew may become later in the evening or more negotiable as the child gets older.

Whatever they are, these nonnegotiable obligations should be accompanied by grace, humor, downtime, and family outings. Teenagers are inconsistent by definition — they mess up and forget; make room for that. Make it fun to be in the family, and make the home a safe refuge, not a grindstone of constant, inflexible tasks.

In the box below, list the nonnegotiables for your family. (Use a separate sheet of paper if you need more space.)

"Battles We Will Fight"

Of the issues discussed above, which ones take highest priority in your family's and teenager's life?

_____

_____

_____

_____

Engage in Conversation

Deuteronomy 6:4–9 is an important passage of Scripture for parents to take to heart. One of the interesting concepts is how constantly you should engage in conversation with your children regarding God's Word. These conversations will give your children the valuable input they need from God and from you regarding this world and how to live for the sake of Christ. Below are three simple ways to keep your conversations going.

First, *constantly check in with your high school student*. Being concerned about the events of your child's daily life is as important at age 16 as it was at age 9, and perhaps more so. Asking how his or her day was or about a specific event or issue gives you a chance to do two things. Your concern gives you a chance to encourage your child and meet any immediate needs. Your teenager may want to be granted some independence but likely doesn't want you to be aloof or unconcerned. If your teenager knows your attitude is one of loving concern for what's going on in his or her daily life, he or she will open up to you, especially if your conversation is accompanied by constant encouragement and "I love yous." Your concern also gives you a chance to mentor your child by lovingly reminding your child of past conversations and principles you have already laid out. This should never be with an "I-told-you-so" attitude but with an attitude to help in processing things. If this habit has been established and pursued since childhood, it teaches a teenager how to be interested and concerned for the lives of others throughout life.

Second, *date your child*. Especially in our culture, where families are going in a dozen different directions, establishing a time every week when *each child* has one-on-one time with *each parent* is essential to keeping conversations going. If you accomplish this every week, fifty-two times a year, you will have had more than two hundred dates (give or take a few) during your child's four years of high school. I bet this outnumbers the items in your lists of wise decision making and warnings you want to talk to him or her about. In these discussions you can broaden the conversation from the nonnegotiables to world events, movies, music, books, and exploring and applying the Scriptures. It will give you a chance to ask your kids about their dreams and aspirations, setting the stage for a robust give-and-take in which you both will grow to know each other and the Savior together.

Third, *engage your child in an investigation of worldviews and apologetics.* Because of the nature of the arguments your children are likely to face when they leave home and enter college or the workforce, it is wise to expose them to the world's arguments while they are under your authority and care. You likely won't find a fair and balanced debate in the public school system, and most Christian schools and youth ministries haven't made this type of education a priority. You can provide your teenagers with the solid biblical answers to the challenges our culture presents, but this will require you to educate yourselves. Some excellent resources are listed at the end of this book to assist you.

Honestly evaluate how well you are doing in these three areas. (Ask for your spouse's opinion, if applicable.)

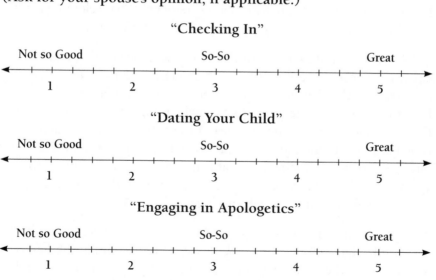

"Checking In"

Not so Good   So-So   Great

1   2   3   4   5

"Dating Your Child"

Not so Good   So-So   Great

1   2   3   4   5

"Engaging in Apologetics"

Not so Good   So-So   Great

1   2   3   4   5

What are one or two things you can do to improve in each of these areas?

Checking In: _____

_____

Dating Your Child: _____

_____

Engaging in Apologetics: _____

_____

Create Significant Experiences

As the ultimate stewards for your children, you can create experiences in their lives to help them realize God's authority and to become more obedient to Christ by being involved together in evangelism and service to others. You can also create experiences that celebrate their growing maturity. Let's explore each of these a little further.

Allow your high school students to make mistakes . . . and to suffer the consequences of their poor choices. And then, *don't bail them out.* Let them wallow in their poor choices and allow them to figure out how they are going to fix, make right, pay for, and change their behavior to avoid such unpleasantness in the future. Much of the time natural consequences are sufficient. But, as a parent, you may have to impose a consequence that is logical to the poor choice that was made. This may inconvenience you; however, the price paid by you is usually worth the result produced.

For example, if it was discovered that my newly licensed and "vehicled" high school son skipped class and hung out at the mall all afternoon, the school would apply a consequence, and so would I. Because we would have already established that the use of the car is to accomplish the *right* things—and skipping school is definitely the wrong thing—I would confiscate the car, say for a week, and set him afoot. Because my child could not be trusted to use the car to go to school and stay at school, I would assume that he hadn't learned that deception is a serious breach of my authority. Now, here's where many parents fail because most teenagers will begin to whine, saying they have early morning band practice every day and work three times a week in the evenings. Our natural inclination is to bail out our children and modify the consequences; after all, the child may lose his or her position in the band or lose a job. Returning to my example, I would explain that these are the consequences he should have thought about *before* skipping school. My teenager would need to find a way to get to band practice and to work without his car. And I would remind him that I won't be available to help him out with this, because it was understood from the beginning that getting a job required having a car. This is what I call a wake-up call for a 16-year-old child who *never* should have skipped school and who most likely won't ever skip school again—especially if there is a history of calm, matter-of-fact discipline. Such discipline reinforces who is in authority and that the responsibility and trust given is expected to be honored in return by using that trust in the right ways. When I return the car keys, I would ask what lessons had been learned and repeat what is expected in the future.

Your preparation for releasing your teenagers should include experiences to help them see the value of serving and sharing their faith. Ask the Lord to open your and your teenagers' eyes to needs in your neighborhood and community, as well as for opportunities to share the gospel. You might also consider a missions trip, especially to a developing nation. This will stretch your children's faith in the Lord and compassion to those in true need.

A family should celebrate significant milestones in their child's life and use these events for praise and encouragement. Some examples may include: making the team after elimination tryouts, earning a driver's license, making straight As (or Bs or Cs if that's your child's capacity), being chosen to display his or her artwork, or winning the blue ribbon for showing a prize lamb at the county fair. Be careful not to compare or pit children against one another, but celebrate each child individually. This is a great way to teach your child to think of others before himself or herself and to rejoice at another's good fortune.

What are you doing to create rich experiences for your high school students in each of the following areas?

Allowing them to make mistakes: _____

_____

_____

Encouraging them to serve and share their faith: _____

_____

_____

Celebrating their achievements: _____

_____

_____

STARTING YOUR JOURNEY
Our child has trusted in Christ as Savior. CHECK! Our child has been carefully and biblically trained. CHECK! Our child is responsive and respectful of authority. CHECK! Our child is ready for a world full of sin and evil. WHOA! WAIT! HOLD ON!

After you've done all you could for your teenager and sent him or her out into the world, your next challenge is to trust God to complete the good work He has started in him or her (Philippians 1:6).

Trusting God

This is a difficult truth for every parent to face, but it must be acknowledged: your children were never yours to begin with—they are God's. Parents are given a fabulous stewardship, but it lasts only for a few years. After that, you must let your child go and trust God, who controls every up and down in your child's life. The parental role shifts to that of a mentor or a friend, and God takes a more prominent role in your child's life.

This becomes an opportunity for you, the parents of high school students, to cling to God in four vital areas.

First, *learn to trust God's plan.* The Lord has all of our days counted (Psalm 139:17) and our steps measured (Proverbs 16:9; 20:24). He has a plan for each person, including your child; you can trust in God's wisdom to bring about the results He desires.

Read the following passages and write down how they might encourage you to trust in God's plan for your child's life.

Proverbs 3:5–6

_____

_____

_____

_____

Matthew 6:25–34

_____

_____

_____

_____

Philippians 1:6

_____

_____

_____

_____

Second, *seek God's grace*. Seek God's grace to help you let go of your child, grace to forgive when he or she makes mistakes, grace to enable you to forget when he or she offends, and grace to listen sincerely.

What does God promise in 2 Corinthians 12:9? How might this help you in preparing your high school student to leave home?

_____

_____

_____

_____

Third, *place your hope in Christ*. Toss aside your worry and fear, and place your hope in Christ, not in your child. Your child will fail at times and his or her life may turn out differently from what you've envisioned, but God knows what He is doing. Hope in Him.

What does Philippians 4:6–7 command us to do?

_____

_____

_____

_____

What is the promise if we obey this command? How important is this to you when it comes to your child?

_____

_____

_____

_____

Fourth, *love with the love of Christ*. Nothing is greater than love. And loving your child with the love of Christ, even when things go awry, is the greatest gift of all.

First Corinthians 13:4–8 lists sixteen characteristics of love. What are they?

1.	9.
2.	10.
3.	11.
4.	12.
5.	13.
6.	14.
7.	15.
8.	16.

Evaluate yourself, either with your spouse or individually. On a scale of 1 to 5 (5 being the best), how well are you doing at expressing each of these four important areas?

Trust	Grace	Hope	Love

What do you need to do to begin cultivating greater trust, grace, hope, and love, both toward your child and toward God, as you get closer to the time that you have to let go?

_____

_____

_____

_____

What Happens if My Child Goes Astray?

God makes no promises as to what your child may do when he or she leaves your home. The sad reality is, rebellion is alive and well. And it begins in some families—even Christian families—while the child is still at home. Rebellion may last a short period of time or a lifetime. No matter the reasons for rebellion, it is heart-wrenching to watch a teenager squander his or her life.

Let me tell you a story. I trusted Christ when I was 15 years old. Because of the way I had been raised, my own bad attitude about church, and what I believed was the lack of an active mentor in my life, I didn't mature in my relationship with Christ. My mouth was just as dirty as it was before I came to know Christ, I *hated* going to church, and I made some choices that led me to the precipice of huge moral mistakes. Though by God's grace I didn't *fall*, for four years my spiritual life was dull. During my sophomore year in college, I met a young woman whom I worked alongside as a dormitory resident assistant, and I had a chance to watch her up close. She was the first peer I had met who had a passionate walk with Jesus Christ. She was authentic, and I wanted what she had—to walk in humility before the Lord.

I was a teenager who wasn't walking with Christ, yet God brought someone into my life who did walk with Christ. And I'm convinced He used her to change my heart. It took someone outside my family to get my attention; it might be the same for your rebellious teen. If you've messed up as a parent and the consequences of your actions have wrought some unpleasant effects on your child's life, hold on to hope. God sees what is needed in your child's life, and He will never cease pursuing him or her.

Were you a rebellious teenager? If so, explain your rebellion.

How does Luke 15:11–24 relate to your story?

_____

_____

_____

_____

Do you have a rebellious teenager? If so, explain his or her rebellion.

_____

_____

_____

_____

How might Luke 15:11–24 encourage you through this time of rebellion?

_____

_____

_____

_____

If your rebellious teen came to his or her "senses" and "returned home," how would you receive him or her? How should you?

_____

_____

_____

_____

Helping your child weather these troubled times takes a holistic approach, calling you to be actively and intimately involved in every area of your teenager's life. No magic formulas can give your child automatic discernment; no instant solutions take the place of constant teaching and consistent discipline; and no walls are high enough to keep out the culture's evil ideas. However, God is faithful. He gives us principles to follow while training our children, the most important of which is teaching our children that authority rests with the Lord. He knows everything we and our high school students need and has our best in mind.

*I*t's *Not* All Relative

Living the Truth as a Christian Single

In those days there was no king in Israel; everyone did what was right in his own eyes.

—*Judges 21:25*

Chapter Six

It's *Not* All Relative
Living the Truth as a Christian Single
by Tony Cammarota

 THE HEART OF THE MATTER
Take a look at the moral landscape of our society, and one word comes to mind: *unpleasant*. The evening news presents little more than a recap of the day's crimes. Murders, assaults, kidnappings, infant abandonment, and sexual perversion have become commonplace news in our day. Local newspapers, cable news stations, and online news sources send the clear message that our society has lost its moral bearings. And even though they still grieve us, stories about lying politicians, embezzling business executives, or adulterous religious leaders no longer surprise us. To make matters worse, much of our culture's entertainment media constantly tells us not only that these things are okay but that we should celebrate them. Movies and television programs are filled with portrayals of one-night stands, sexual escapades of hip singles, and singles living together because "that is just what dating couples do these days." In such an environment, we have adopted the mind-set or philosophy known as moral relativism. Chuck Swindoll discerned this and described it in chapter 1 in his list of the lies our world has bought into: "*No rules are valid.* This means that we should make up our own minds about right and wrong, only obeying those things we feel are right for us. In other words, if it feels right, do it" (page 12).

Without a doubt, we live in an age of moral relativism, an age that says basic principles of right and wrong behavior are based on something that can change. One person may base his morals purely on feelings. Another may ground her morals in a culture's ever-changing social norms. Other singles may derive their morals from the idea that "as long as you don't hurt anybody, then it's okay." For example, "Sex before marriage is okay because we love each other and we are not hurting each other." Sadly, in our world many call evil good and good evil. And from their perspective, why not? If the grounding for all morals can change, then our standards of morality can change as well.

What are some ways that you have observed our culture's embrace of moral relativism? More specifically, how have you seen singles live out the lie of moral relativism?

_____

_____

_____

_____

Have you seen the evidence of moral relativism in your own life? In what ways?

_____

_____

_____

_____

It shouldn't surprise us that many of those who don't profess to have a relationship with Jesus Christ propagate moral relativism. Why would we expect them to think or act any differently? If their hearts remain darkened by sin, then they will live accordingly. Even though this shift to moral relativism is troubling, the real heartache lies in the reality that so many who profess to have a personal relationship with Jesus Christ act just like their non-believing friends. In fact, many born-again believers have embraced the concept of moral relativism, making moral choices based solely on feelings and inclinations rather than on the clear teaching of God's Word.

In her book *Real Sex: The Naked Truth about Chastity*, Lauren F. Winner honestly told her personal story about sex outside of marriage. She described her journey as a born-again believer who began with so-called biblical validation for her position on the issues. In her thinking, those feelings of love she experienced validated a sexual relationship outside of marriage. Over time and with a second look at Scripture, she realized that sex is for the marriage relationship only, regardless of whether or not two unmarried people love each other. After this discovery, she now tells singles to base their decisions on what the Bible teaches, not on our shifting, often complex emotions.[1]

Describe a time when you based an important decision on something other than a biblical foundation. What reasons did you give for making that decision?

_____

_____

_____

Recent research bears out the influence of moral relativism in the church, revealing a small difference between the lifestyles of born-again Christians and non-Christians. When pollsters asked born-again Christian Americans about their activities during a typical month, they were *just as likely* as non-born-again adults to steal, consult a psychic, physically fight or abuse someone, use illegal drugs, lie, take revenge, or slander another person.[2]

David Kinnaman and Gabe Lyons—expanding on a study performed by the Barna Group that compared younger Christians, those born between 1965 and 1983 (called "Busters"), with their over-40 counterparts (called "pre-Busters)—wrote that

> just 5 percent of born-again Busters say they have recently given someone "the finger." But compared to this vulgar gesture, *born-again Christian* young people are *three times* more likely to have had sex outside of marriage in the last month (18 percent), *five times* more likely to have gotten drunk (24 percent), and

five times more likely to have purchased a lottery ticket (25 percent). They hold up their middle finger *much less* frequently than they use profanity in public (36 percent), view explicit sexual content in a magazine or a movie (36 percent), or say mean things about others (40 percent).[3]

Yes, our world has adopted and is celebrating a self-focused morality. Let's be honest; living as a single person can easily perpetuate a mind-set of "me." With this perspective, Christian singles can unwittingly embrace this self-centered moral relativism, making it more acceptable than ever to live a life of sin in the church.

In spite of this growing problem, be encouraged. A dark reality is nothing new. And remember, things *can* change.

 DISCOVERING THE WAY
Looking back at Israel's history in the Old Testament, we find a season when Israel embraced moral relativism.

It's Nothing New

During the years between Joshua's death and the rise of Israel's kings, men and women called judges ruled God's people. For approximately three hundred years, the nation plunged itself into a vicious cycle. It began when the Israelites would turn away from following God, resulting in God's discipline through the oppression of the Israelites by other nations. Next, the people would cry out to God for help, pleading for God to send them a deliverer—a judge—to lead them back to peace. But then, after God's gracious deliverance, they would again turn away from following God, continuing the cycle over and over again.

 Read Judges 17:1–6; 21:25.

According to these verses, what reason did the author give for the people's descent into the sin of idolatry?

_____

_____

_____

What did the Israelites use as their guiding compass of morality?

_____

_____

_____

"Every man did what was right in his own eyes" summarizes the cultural mores in both ancient Israel's day and ours. If you take some time to read through the entire book of Judges you'll discover murder, idolatry, lying, adultery, materialism, and so much more. Sounds a lot like our newscasts, doesn't it? Were Hollywood to make the book of Judges into a movie, it would have to be an R-rated film. At the root of such moral decay was the people's belief that they themselves were the standard of morality. Each individual derived his or her moral bearings solely from within, embracing once again the lie that Satan told Eve: "and you will be like God" (Genesis 3:5). The Israelites gave in to this temptation throughout their history, and so do we. The desire to be our own god has consumed us from the beginning of humanity.

Why do you think Satan's words to Eve in Genesis 3:1–6 were so appealing?

_____

_____

_____

As a single person, what are some examples of messages that you receive from movies, magazines, or music about what you should do in life that are both appealing and contrary to Scripture? Why are they so appealing to you?

_____

_____

_____

_____

According to Romans 1:18–32, once people begin ignoring the truth, what do they begin to do?

_____

_____

_____

What happens to them?

_____

_____

_____

What similarities do you see between these biblical scenarios (Genesis 3, Judges, and Romans 1) and our current cultural expression of moral relativism?

_____

_____

_____

_____

All people encounter the sinful desire to suppress the truth about God. Do you remember the first time you saw a toy jack-in-the-box? As the handle cranked around and around, the music played. After some time, the clown surprisingly popped out of the box. Then someone pushed the "jack" back into the box, closed the lid, and acted as though nothing ever came out of the box—only to do it all over again. This is what humans can do. We push the truth about God back into the box, pretending like it never appeared. Romans 1 tells us that people do this because of their unrighteousness. In other words, we suppress truth because we want to be "like God." We do not want anybody or any Being telling us what we should or should not do. After all, have we not been told that we are the masters of our own fate?

After God gives humans up to the lusts of their hearts, dishonorable passions, and a debased mind, aberrant behavior inevitably follows. In Romans 1:32, we observe that the end result of moral relativism lends us the hearty approval of those who practice morally compromised lifestyles.

What Not to Do

So for those who have been saved by God's grace, where do we start? How can we stem the tide of moral decay? How can we positively influence the world in which we live? Here are several things we should *not* do.

First, *we should not get mad at the world*. Christians really have no business self-righteously telling non-Christians how bad they are. Many well-meaning Christians have adopted this hypocritical approach. Unfortunately, this has done more harm than good. The Pharisees in Jesus's day did this. And it was the Pharisees who received Jesus's sharpest criticism.

Second, *we should not simply tell Christians to "be more moral."* Believers have been preaching this for decades, especially to the younger generation. But the reality of morally relativistic lifestyles exhibited by younger Christians demonstrates that the message "be more moral" just isn't getting the job done. Telling singles what to do without telling them why or how hasn't had its intended effect.

Many believe that the most important thing about being a Christian is to be a moral person. When Christians were asked in a study to identify the main priorities of the Christian faith, their answers were staggering: "being good, doing the right thing, not sinning."[4] But is "being good" really the main thing? From the pages of the New Testament, the most important thing is to love God and love others. Jesus Himself said the mark of a Christian is not his or her morals but the Christian's love for others (John 13:34–35). It seems that Christians have been telling the world *and themselves* that morality is the main thing. However, neither Christian nor non-Christian lifestyles have been affected much by that singular message.

Third, *we should not shelter ourselves from the "big bad world with big bad people."* As a single person, it is tempting to try to isolate oneself from the evil in the world. One can wake in the morning alone, go to work with limited interaction with others, then come home to spend leisure time alone. And so the routine goes day after day. Lack of significant relationships is never healthy. Singles are to be on guard from isolating themselves from other believers and particularly from a culture in which we are called to be salt and light.

This is a good time to pause and think about your current approach to moral relativism. Do you consider it a pervasive problem? Take a moment to write down what you have done personally to address this issue. Have your efforts made a positive contribution, or have they perpetuated a problem?

_____

_____

_____

_____

So what is the next step?

STARTING YOUR JOURNEY
Despite the dark reality of ever-shifting morals, we need
not despair. We may feel hopeless, beat down, lonely, or
apathetic, but there is no need to live that way.

It Can Change

On the contrary, Jesus Christ left us with His Word and His Spirit to
navigate us through the tough times. Single Christians were never
meant to live their lives waiting to fully live until they get married.
Rather, the years of living as a single Christian can be some of the most
spiritually fruitful of one's life. In the pages of the New Testament
are found two starting points for Christians: one that will influence
our own lives and one that will help us positively influence the morally relativistic world in which we live.

 Read Luke 18:9–14.

To whom did Jesus tell this parable?

_____

_____

What was the lesson that Jesus intended them to learn?

_____

_____

_____

God commends the humble, not those who have a self-righteous
arrogance (see also 1 Peter 5:5). The Pharisee of Luke 18 compared
himself with others, thanking God that he was not like "other people."
He trusted his external religious behaviors and his abstinence from
immoral behavior to earn God's favor (Luke 18:11–12). This proud
disposition is self-deceiving, and it turns away both God and others.

The tax collector, on the other hand, admitted the reality of his position. He knew others saw him as a leech and a traitor. Rather than prompting him to recount the good deeds he had done for God, this honesty with himself and with God drove him to acknowledge his status as a sinner in need of mercy. He resisted comparisons between himself and others because he saw God as his primary audience. Likewise, we do not look to other humans as our moral standard. Having another human as our moral standard will never work because that person is always changing, just as we are. He or she will always be a moving target of morality. That is why Christian singles must not take their moral cues from movies, music, or celebrities that present some façade of a great life.

For the Christian seeking to avoid the trap of moral relativism, our first step is to model our lives after the tax collector and not the Pharisee. To make any significant impact in a morally relativistic society, we must first be honest with ourselves and with God about our own sinfulness and our need for a Savior. In appropriate ways, Christians must honestly acknowledge their sin to God and to others. We must not put on the pretense that we have it all together. We must not look down on others with a smug attitude of moral superiority. And we must admit that if God had not stepped into our lives with His amazing grace, we, too, would certainly do "what was right in [our] own eyes" (Judges 21:25). As we walk the path of authenticity, we will soon see the fruits of our positive influence in a world that has lost its way.

 Read 1 Timothy 1:15.

Paul wrote this after being a Christian approximately twenty-five years. What continued to be his main message?

_____

_____

_____

_____

How did Paul see himself?

_____

_____

_____

Paul continued to tell others about the gospel decades after his first encounter with Christ. As we seek to stand firm in a relativistic society, we, too, need to live out the gospel and tell others about our Lord. By doing this, we will impact the dark world in which we live. We must boldly and graciously tell others that Jesus Christ came to save sinners. And when we tell them this, we must admit that we are the ones most in need. We cannot budge on clearly defining right and wrong, but when we point out the boundary lines, we must do it in a redemptive way, not a condemning one. Christ came to save sinners, not to condemn them or shame them or "put them in their place." In all the truth He lived out and spoke about, He was always redemptive. With Jesus, the moral lines were clear.

Despite what the culture conveys, Christian singles are called to live authentically. It is possible! You can admit reality and do the hard work of being honest with yourself. With maturity and discretion, you can reveal your brokenness to others. Authenticity means you do not compromise on moral standards but simply acknowledge that you have broken them personally and sometimes frequently. And you go a step further and cherish what Jesus Christ has done on your behalf; that is, He came to save sinners. In a culture that frowns upon truth, Christian singles living as humble examples are a powerful testimony to the power and reality of Christ.

Jesus's purpose was to save. His intentions were to make all things new. He did not approach the moral decay with pride and bitterness. Rather, He grieved. He reached out. He showed grace. And He did this because He loves us. Our task as His followers is to say what He said and to live like He did.

Dr. Mark Young, president of Denver Seminary, has often said, "We have no right to be right unless we are redemptive." Christians have been entrusted with truth that does not change. As we grow in our relationship with Christ, we understand this truth more clearly and apply it more faithfully. However, God never intended His gift of truth to make us prideful. Rather, knowing who God is, who we are, and what God has spoken about morality should always lead us to a lifestyle of love and redemption.

This approach truly brings hope to our troubled world.

What about Tolerance?
What to Stand For, and
When to Stand

Chapter Seven

What about Tolerance?
What to Stand For, and When to Stand
by Terry Boyle

THE HEART OF THE MATTER

We nostalgically refer to the past as a simpler time. And that may be true. Today's world is a complicated place.

Due to advances in communication and travel, we find ourselves thinking globally now. We face troubles and learn of crises that cross not only national borders but continental borders as well. On a daily basis, we encounter people with different backgrounds, different priorities, and different mind-sets. One of them might even be sitting across the breakfast table from you! Nowadays, more and more marriages are composed of spouses from different parts of the globe . . . and, even if not literally, it may often seem that way.

With so many conflicting views and philosophies out there for us to take in and consider, is it fair or reasonable to claim that certain ways are right, while others are wrong? Shouldn't we just do our best to get along? Isn't tolerance the golden key to a peaceful life? Isn't tolerance the godly way, after all?

DISCOVERING THE WAY

This question of tolerance as a godly virtue has two aspects to it: cultural tolerance and moral tolerance.

With cultural tolerance, we see many variations between cultures and societies. We enjoy traveling as tourists to other regions and countries in the interest of exploring these variations.

As an Englishman living in rural Texas for many years, I took a while to get used to iced tea, pickup trucks, and rodeos. But that was the culture, and it wasn't to be judged as right or wrong—it just *was*. In fact, I still really enjoy it. One of my most endearing and enduring memories was the time I asked my youth group to help me brainstorm for our next fundraiser. One of them jumped up—you might know one just like him: yoked Navajo-print shirt, narrow jeans, a big silver belt buckle, and roper boots—and offered his suggestion: "We could go out one night and shoot some wild hogs, then butcher 'em and sell the meat door-to-door!" His remained the most original suggestion that particular Wednesday night, and I'd take it over another car wash any day. As they say: "Nowhar but Texas." Differences like that are neither moral nor ethical—they're cultural. And we can tolerate, even celebrate, them in this shrinking world of ours.

The way you were reared is *never* identical to the way your spouse was brought up—we all bring different cultural cards to the table. That's part of what makes life fun. To you, a normal family might be loud and chaotic and expressive—by way of example, imagine for a moment growing up New York Italian. But if your partner grew up in a quiet, rural place where the loudest sound was the buzz of a cricket or the turning of a book page, then you might need to negotiate a new "normal" between the two of you. In cases like that, cultural tolerance can be foundational to the relationship, because neither of you is wrong—you just *are*.

But moral tolerance is another matter. Here we deal with our attitude toward those issues that run counter to God's declared plan for humanity. In other words, we're talking about tolerance toward sin. Is moral tolerance a godly virtue?

Let's not confuse tolerance with patience. Tolerance refers to the idea of overlooking or ignoring an issue—either pretending it isn't wrong or just not believing it to be so. But God isn't *tolerant* of sin. He never pretends to overlook any sin, nor does He sugarcoat it. Rather, He exacts a very full penalty for it. The question has to do with how long God will wait, and, ultimately, who bears the penalty.

Ancient Israel fell more than once into the error of believing that God was tolerant of sin. The book of Judges recounts time and time again how they prospered under God's blessing for a while and then in time forgot about His standards and "did evil in the sight of the LORD" (Judges 2:11; 3:7; 4:1; 6:1; 10:6; 13:1). In the gracious plan of God, He always offers the opportunity to repair our relationship with Him through repentance. We see this pattern repeated in Judges, as God sent enemies against Israel to get their attention and remind them of their obligations to His holiness. The nation would repent and return to God's ways for a while before the next cycle began.

It's worth reminding ourselves that God's patience in no way means that He will not judge sin. Peter discussed this idea in the context of God's intention to judge the earth and the ungodly with consuming fire.

 Read 2 Peter 3:9–11.

The message of the Bible is plain and straightforward: we can escape from God's judgment against sin only through Christ. Sins do not go unpunished; rather, God graciously removes them from our account through the cross. In Christ, God promises to forgive our sins, not pretend that we were never guilty in the first place (Matthew 26:28; Ephesians 1:7). By the way, nothing is wrong with telling others that we believe this. It is an honest expression of biblical truth. To speak these words often earns Christians the brand of religious intolerance because the gospel is, at its core, divisive. Some go to judgment, some go to glory, yet we receive scorn for saying it plainly.

While we can suffer hard times as a result of speaking the truth, we also face greater danger: the danger of abusing God's promise of forgiveness and turning it into an excuse to do whatever we want. Sometimes we tend to take God's grace for granted. Certainly, He is quick to forgive, but should we really rely on His mercy as a license to indulge ourselves? The repetitive cycle of sin and repentance, sin and repentance may be a symptom of religious complacency. This confuses God's *patience* with our *tolerance*.

Though we can see it clearly in others, often this cycle of indulgence and tolerance can be hidden within the circle of the home . . . and the effects are devastating. Outbursts of rage with emotional and even physical harm often occur in this pattern, as well as spending sprees, substance abuse, and sexual infidelity. Something happens and harm is done. An apology is issued—even a really convincing one—but then the whole cycle starts again and the same pattern plays out once more.

Read Isaiah 1:10–17, where God addressed the people of Israel as if they were Sodom and Gomorrah (two cities God destroyed because of their sin; see Genesis 19), and answer the following questions.

Who gave the sacrificial system to Israel?

_____

_____

What was the common function of the sacrifice (see Leviticus 1:3–4)?

_____

_____

_____

_____

Why do you think God was so frustrated with His people in Isaiah 1?

_____

_____

_____

_____

Rather than keep bringing sacrifices — "trampling His courts" — for their continued sin, what would God prefer?

_____

_____

_____

Now compare Romans 6:1–4 in the New Testament. Has God's attitude toward sin changed in any way since the final sacrifice of Christ? Describe His attitude in this passage.

_____

_____

_____

STARTING YOUR JOURNEY

In the opening chapter of this book, Chuck Swindoll described the troubling areas of our world: "the politics of our day, the spiritual apathy of our culture, and the directionless, hopeless, and immoral morass that the great majority of our world finds itself in today" (page 6). The chapters in this book are designed to give you some direction, some biblical grounding, for how to live out your faith in a world that seems to be slipping quickly away from its moorings.

How Should We Respond?

Nothing happens in this world that does not have God's hand over it. It may well be that He is reshaping nations before our eyes. Certainly the events of our times bring to mind the biblical descriptions of a world in decline. Our first human reaction might be to duck and cover, to hide out until the storm has passed. Then, on reflection, we might quickly sanctify that selfish impulse with a brave commitment to persevere through the storm, gritting our teeth and clinging tightly to God as our anchor. But I propose going one step further as families face uncertainty in a world that is becoming less and less family-friendly.

If God is bringing about change, even hardship and difficulty, we can do more than just hang on and wait for the storm to blow over. Six centuries before Christ's incarnation, Jerusalem and Judah eventually wore out God's patience and fell under His hand of judgment. God raised up the Babylonians to use as a whip against the unfaithful Judeans. All this was in keeping with God's covenant promises to Israel, as spoken through Moses some eight hundred years earlier.

 Read Habakkuk 1:1–17.

The prophet Habakkuk wrote during the time leading up to Babylon's invasion of Judah, and the first four verses of this passage constitute his "state of the nation" address. Habakkuk complained that God seemed to overlook or even ignore the sins of His people.

What seems to have been Judah's general condition at that time (Habakkuk 1:3–4)?

_____

_____

_____

_____

Habakkuk spoke of violence and strife in Judah. According to verse 4, what are the moral and social consequences?

_____

_____

_____

_____

Habakkuk 1:5–11 describes God's response to Habakkuk's complaint. How do you imagine the prophet received the news at first? Why?

_____

_____

_____

_____

According to Habakkuk 3:16–19, what was Habakkuk's response ultimately?

_____

_____

_____

_____

Not *everyone* from Judah was evil; Daniel, Shadrach, Meshach, and Abed-nego, and also the prophets Jeremiah and Ezekiel, were alive at this time. In light of this, do you think God promises "convenience" for the righteous? Why, or why not?

_____

_____

_____

_____

Habakkuk, a prophet who understood the times, was able to perceive and understand God's acts of judgment while speaking in faith as he watched and waited for the inevitable disaster. Did you notice the prophet's reaction to impending disaster? Because he knew that God was behind the shaking of the nations (even his own nation), he could *exult* and *rejoice*. We can do so much more than just hunker down and hang on in the face of sin. We can praise God, and we can stand up for righteousness.

 Read 1 Corinthians 6:9–11.

Notice that Paul did not tiptoe around the prior sins of the congregation at Corinth; he listed them plainly (1 Corinthians 6:9–10). He made it clear that their old ways were behind them (6:11). We, too, are to be different from the world, even while we live in it. The Bible calls upon us to walk as light, having been redeemed from darkness (Ephesians 5:8).

What steps can you take in your marriage and family life to humbly expose sin and walk in grace? Search your heart and consider your own life first.

_____

_____

_____

The following are just a few additional ideas.

- Give your spouse free access to your computer at any time. Use it in the family room, not in secret.

- Set house rules about what television programs you will and will not watch. Let the scruples of the most sensitive partner set the level. Look after your spouse, and don't cause him or her to regret spending leisure time with you just because the show you wanted to watch was tacky. If a particular show consistently crosses the line, write to the station and tell them you are no longer watching their program and why.

- On the subject of letter-writing, don't forget to contact the editor of your local newspaper and your local and national governmental representatives regarding the significant issues of our day.

- Express yourself through the marketplace. Especially in times of economic stress, marketers are sensitive to opinions. If you find a particular ad campaign morally offensive, don't buy the product and make sure you let the company's executives at the highest level possible know why.

- Establish rules beforehand, in a non-argumentative way, concerning guests in your home. Agree on the rules and work out together how you will communicate with guests. Couples can drift into awkward situations with visiting guests and family by not being clear as to what is and is not tolerated in your home. Support each other so that guests don't play you against each other.

When couples communicate a united front against immorality, the world outside pays attention. God calls us to be salt and light, winsome and helpful to others as we live out a better way. Paul said living a life apart from sinners is impossible because we would have to leave this world to achieve that (1 Corinthians 5:9–10). The Bible provides wisdom and insight into how we can live a dignified and sanctified life, even in a world of sin.

Because moral tolerance is not a godly virtue (despite the clamor of the world to the contrary), we do not need to condone or ignore sin. We can, as Paul put it, "stand firm against the schemes of the devil" (Ephesians 6:11). Without being harsh or vindictive, we can take a firm position and hold to it. Bear in mind that the last thing we need is one of those legalistic bullet-lists that proves our righteousness to the world or to our spouse. None of us has bragging rights. Christ redeemed us all from the mess we're in. Let's practice cultural tolerance by accepting our differences while we stand firm for God's holy moral standards.

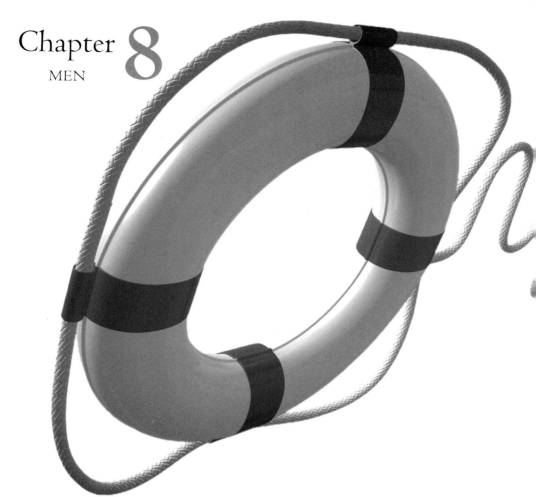

Chapter **8**
MEN

$\mathcal{A}$ Leader Worth Following

A Man Who Follows Christ

Have this attitude in yourselves which was also in Christ Jesus, who, although He existed in the form of God, did not regard equality with God a thing to be grasped, but emptied Himself, taking the form of a bond-servant, and being made in the likeness of men.

Chapter Eight

A Leader Worth Following
A Man Who Follows Christ
by Les Fleetwood

THE HEART OF THE MATTER

Here's the understatement of the year: now, more than ever, it's hard to be a godly man. Surprised? Of course not! Thanks to ubiquitous technology, we men who claim Christ as Savior receive daily bombardment by hundreds, if not thousands, of nonbiblical images and opinions of manliness, strength, leadership, and success. Satan attempts to marginalize the importance and minimize the impact of godly men through certain avenues and attitudes of our culture, such as:

- *Style over Substance*: preferring the superficial to that which has depth.

- *Charisma over Character*: confusing likability and eloquence for authenticity and integrity.

- *Fame over Fidelity*: crowning flashiness and image as king while forgetting or even mocking faithfulness.

- *Rights over Responsibilities*: getting our way becomes more important than doing the right thing.

- *Self-promotion over Servanthood*: in workplaces around the nation, "success at all costs" rules the day, while people end up considering sacrifice and service quaint and irrelevant. Time and time again we hear the world telling us: "What you believe is right! Do whatever it takes to reach your goals!"

It's bad enough to see our culture saturated with this kind of thinking, but it's worse when it sneaks its way into the church, further confusing men who seek to lead godly lives. Countless preachers teach us to treat our faith like some magic wand to conjure up whatever we desire. And not to lay full blame on others, each of us can get into trouble on our own! Even the great apostle Paul admitted to the weaknesses of his sinful nature (Romans 7:15–25).

And let's not forget the unintentional confusion we run into in men's ministry. Are you experiencing spiritual fatigue from the myriad of books, articles, and pumped-up weekend conferences promoting one form or another of "muscular" Christianity? You know what I'm talking about. Words like *warrior* and *wild* are thrown around. A lot. This message to men is powerful and well-meaning, but aren't we looking for something a little less strenuous and a lot more straightforward when it comes to being a godly leader?

List some of the ways you've observed the following values play out in our culture: style over substance, charisma over character, fame over fidelity, rights over responsibilities, and self-promotion over servanthood. Evaluate the results from a Christian perspective.

_____

_____

_____

_____

Have you noticed these compromised values within your local church or in the lives of Christian men you know?

_____

_____

_____

In what situations have you been tempted to do whatever it takes to reach your goals?

_____

_____

_____

 DISCOVERING THE WAY

Every morning upon entering my office at the church, my eyes land on a little blue sign on the window ledge. And every morning I read and reflect on these words written upon it:

> Resolved, that I will live so, as I shall wish I had done when I come to die.

This resolution, penned in 1722 by the great theologian and preacher Jonathan Edwards, captures the core desire of most Christian men with whom I've ministered. We long to know God better and to do those things that are right and good, to pursue the things that honor Him. We don't concern ourselves with being wild warriors as much as with being faithful husbands, loving fathers, loyal friends, and ethical businessmen.

We strive to be real men, authentic in our leadership; men of our word who say what we mean and mean what we say; men who take care of the details with integrity. We long to be men who pray more, men who trust and obey God more.

Simply put, we desire to lead lives that make our heavenly Father proud and to lead others in these same ways.

Follow the Leader

So, what does it take to become a leader worth following? It's been said that great leaders are also great followers. If so, we'd first better make sure we're following the right person! And if we want to become a godly leader, who better to follow than Jesus Himself?

 Read Philippians 2:5–11.

In this passage, we discover the worthiness of following Jesus because He is:

- *Sovereign:* Jesus is coequal and coeternal with God the Father (Philippians 2:6).

- *Sympathetic:* Jesus understands our human condition because He also became fully human (2:6–7).

- *A Servant:* The crucifixion of Jesus on our behalf stands as the ultimate model of servanthood, humility, and obedience (2:7–8).

- *Our Savior and Lord:* God's resurrection and exaltation of Jesus demands our worship (2:9–11).

According to Philippians 2:5–11, what are the foundational attitudes and resulting actions of Christ?

_____

_____

_____

Taking Christ's example in Philippians 2:5–11, what are some practical ways we men can become more Christlike in our leadership at home, church, and on the job?

_____

_____

_____

_____

Read Romans 12:3.

What attitude did Paul encourage us to embrace?

_____

_____

How does Romans 12:3 relate to the passage you just read in Philippians?

_____

_____

Why can this attitude be tough to model on the job?

_____

_____

_____

As long as I live, I'll never forget Greg Hatteberg. Greg was my boss when I worked at Dallas Theological Seminary, but to call him my boss would be grossly insufficient. He was a model of Christlike servant-leadership who impacted my life in many ways. Here are just a few:

- He showed me that a leader can and should show individuals concern and compassion. I will never forget his daily words of encouragement.

- He taught me that it's okay to laugh . . . and that if it's done loudly it will make more people happy.

- He reminded me to love God and others and commit to the local church.

- He modeled how a godly dad treats his kids.

- He taught me how a husband should love his wife . . . unconditionally, as Christ "loved the church and gave Himself up for her" (Ephesians 5:25).

- He exemplified true humility by living the adage, "People won't see or hear Christ if we're standing in the way."

Which men in your life modeled godly leadership worth following? Why do you remember them? What did they say or do that impacted your life?

_____

_____

_____

Godly leadership doesn't grasp for position and power. Rather, it sacrifices and serves. Our calling to be godly leaders in our homes, in our churches, and on our jobs presents us with a serious challenge when our culture continuously cries out, "What you believe is right! Do anything to achieve your goals!" But we must remind ourselves that a leader worth following is a leader following Christ.

Signposts of Godly Leadership

Proverbs 3:5–6 contains four signposts directing us to helpful principles for godly leadership. We'll take a look at each one.

 Read Proverbs 3:5–6.

What is the first command in verse 5?

_____

_____

_____

The Hebrew word *batach*, "trust," in verse 5 "expresses that sense of well-being and security which results from having something or someone in whom to place confidence."[1] So to "trust in the Lord" means to rely upon Him for strength and support. Imagine it! The Creator of the universe is also our Sustainer. As Christian men, our security and stability in life come from our personal relationship with and reliance on God.

What is the level of commitment required in this command? What are some ways you can achieve this level of commitment?

_____

_____

_____

Signpost One: Complete security in the Lord requires complete submission to the Lord.

Scripture portrays the heart as the seat of one's emotions, an image of a person's entire being. Proverbs 3:5 requires no shallow trust from us, for it commands us to trust with *all* our hearts, meaning our entire lives — emotions, intellect, will — *everything*! A leader worth following has taken a humble step down.

What is the second command in verse 5?

_____

_____

_____

How does that second command contrast with the first? Why do you think the contrast is significant?

_____

_____

_____

Signpost Two: Human intellect can never replace godly insight.

Proverbs 3:5b emphasizes that we must rely on God, not ourselves. Our own understanding and intellect cannot match the wisdom of God. Consistently listen to God speak to you as you read and apply His Word. A leader worth following saturates his mind and life with the Scriptures.

What is the third command (verse 6a)?

_____

_____

_____

In the Hebrew text, the term "acknowledge Him" highlights the preeminence of God in our lives. The Hebrew root *yada*, "acknowledge," contains the ideas of confessing and giving praise and thanks to God, as we declare His greatness.[2] This word, then, points to essential elements in a believer's personal relationship with God.

The Message paraphrases Proverbs 3:6, "Listen for God's voice in everything you do, everywhere you go." How does this rendering add to your understanding of what it means to "acknowledge God"?

_____

_____

_____

Signpost Three: Intentional surrender to the Lord leads to thankful praise to the Lord.

Every day, share your life with God. He knows all about you already, but He wants you to come to Him willingly. Share every aspect of your life with Him: your dreams, doubts, desires, disappointments, decisions, deeds, and duties. Confess your sin. Receive His forgiveness. Enjoy His grace. A leader worth following experiences the fullness of God in everything he does and everywhere he goes.

When we obey the three commands in Proverbs 3:5–6a, state in your own words the principle that results in verse 6b.

_____

_____

_____

_____

For the longest time, this verse brought to my mind the image of God picking up my crooked path of life like a rope by the ends and pulling it until it straightened out. That was how I understood and envisioned God "making my paths straight." But that's not the idea here. The Hebrew word *yashar*, translated to "make . . . straight," means to "make smooth or straight, i.e. free from obstacles, successful." [3]

Life isn't always easy. Christ Himself said, "In the world you have tribulation" (John 16:33). How can we reconcile this with our understanding of the Hebrew words in Proverbs 3:6b, that He will make our paths "smooth, free from obstacles, successful"?

_____

_____

_____

_____

If we understand "success" to mean "spiritual health and growth," how might you interpret verse 6b?

_____

_____

_____

_____

Signpost Four: Godly leaders let God lead.

Why? Because they realize He's in charge. He's in control. We sometimes like to think that we control our lives . . . until we hit a major crisis. Then we realize how out of control our lives really are when left in our hands.

Now, don't misunderstand. This is a proverb—a principle—not a promise. God doesn't promise us an easy life of smooth sailing. Instead, Proverbs 3:5–6 teaches a general rule of thumb: when we completely submit ourselves to God, relying on His wisdom over our own, and when we draw near to Him in confession, praise, and thanksgiving, we can be confident that He will guide us, keeping our lives on track by either completely removing difficulties or by leaving them where they are and helping us navigate through them. We can trust that He will send someone to help us carry the load or strengthen us to carry the load in His strength. A leader worth following has experienced life's difficulties yet still testifies of God's faithfulness.

STARTING YOUR JOURNEY

Most Christian men I know have the same desire: they truly long to be God's man—to be a real man, an authentic man, a man who leads his family with love and strength, a man who leads his church with passion and purpose, and a man who leads in the marketplace with integrity.

Have you been burned by other men posing as leaders? In what ways did they disappoint? What can you do to avoid becoming like them? What is God asking you to do?

_____

_____

_____

So you want to be a leader worth following? Not just someone who flashes style and charisma, but a godly leader who cares about substance and character?

What are those things of substance, character, and fidelity that you desire for your life?

_____

_____

_____

What prevents you from pursuing them? To whom can you turn for help?

_____

_____

_____

⸭

Because a leader worth following is a leader following Christ, here's your challenge from our study of Philippians 2 and Proverbs 3:

Renew your commitment to Christ today. Live for Him whole-heartedly, not necessarily as some wild warrior but as an authentic leader who has taken a humble step down. Saturate your mind and life with the Scriptures. Experience the fullness of God—His grace, power, mercy, love, forgiveness—in everything you do and everywhere you go. Be a leader who has experienced life's difficulties yet still testifies of God's faithfulness.

If you do these things humbly before God, then, like Jonathan Edwards, you will live the life you always have wished to live. You will become a leader worth following.

Between Love and Judgment

A Christian Woman's War

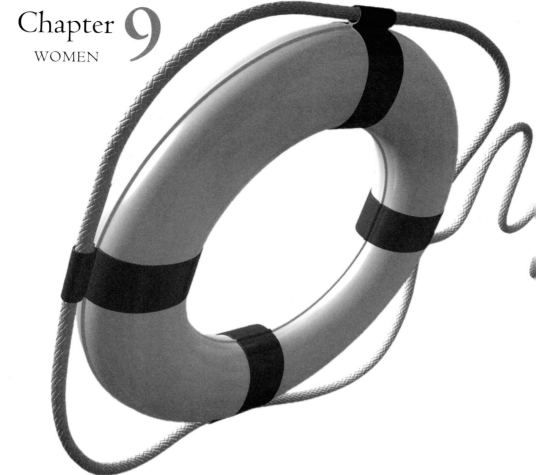

s not those w
ick. But go a
acrifice,' for I

Chapter Nine

Between Love and Judgment
A Christian Woman's War
by Brianna Barrier Engeler

THE HEART OF THE MATTER
Most people in our society who do not know Christ have a negative view of Christians and the church. Can you blame them?

In a society where the cardinal virtue—the one trumpeted by the media above all others—is tolerance, any semblance of right or wrong is quickly dismissed. When the line between right and wrong is erased and morality is determined on a case-by-case basis, any form of judgment or statement of absolute truth is translated as meaningless rejection or hypocrisy.

As Christian women, we are tasked with an incredibly daunting challenge: How can we authentically love those around us without compromising our biblical values? Are we condoning sin by not confronting it? Is it our job to judge? Or to love? Or to do both?

The answer lies in living an authentic life modeled after Jesus Christ. He didn't stay away from unbelievers and sinners in the name of purity. He called out sin wherever He saw it—but His ultimate motivation was love.

DISCOVERING THE WAY
Crinkled into a thousand sparkling bits of tinfoil, my hair resembled a giant aluminum sculpture . . . or Sputnik; take your pick. I was at the mercy of my new hairstylist, held captive in her chair by a burning sensation on my scalp and a desire to hide my face from the world until this horrific beauty ritual ended.

We had about forty-five minutes to kill, so I searched for a scintillating topic of conversation. "So, tell me about you," I said. Okay, not my most eloquent moment.

She hesitated for a moment, and then she began to tell me her story. This spunky, lovely young woman had spent the last twelve years of her life as a hard-core methamphetamine addict. A few months ago, she joined Narcotics Anonymous, and she was celebrating her first ninety days of sobriety on the next Saturday.

When I asked her what had drawn her to confront her addiction, she commented, "I drove by the church down the street. I'd never gone in before; I've always thought that Christians were judgmental hypocrites and avoided them at all costs. But for some reason, I just had to get out of the car. When I did, I ran into the youth pastor's wife. She told me about Jesus, and I asked Him to forgive me and to love me right then and there."

My reaction of joy was quickly tempered as she then poured out her heart about her live-in boyfriend and the fact that he wouldn't marry her. She said she would have left him, "but the sex is amazing, and I just have needs. We all do, you know?"

I didn't know how to respond. I froze. Here was a hurting, fragile person who I sensed deeply desired my approval. After all, she was finally sober, and she had just trusted Christ as her Savior. But she wanted me to tell her that this other area of her life was okay for the moment; that it would eventually work out; that she didn't need to give up this part of her old self yet.

Frankly, I blew it. I was terrified that if I opened my mouth to mention my concerns, she would dismiss me as another judgmental hypocrite and maybe even be angry enough to return to her addiction. So I just sat there—torn between my desire to love her and my tendency to judge her—until it was time to walk out the door.

Choosing to Live in the Real World

In Jesus's day, tax collectors were reviled—not just disliked but actively hated. The Roman government enlisted these men to implement heavy taxation, and the people resented it. Plus, the average tax collector used his position to line his own pockets. So most Jews considered these men—including Matthew the tax collector—as crooks or thieves to be avoided at all costs.

 Read Matthew 9:9–13.

When Jesus first saw Matthew, what did He say? How did Matthew respond? From what you know from the rest of the Scriptures, who did Matthew become and what was his legacy?

_____

_____

_____

Can you imagine that the Pharisees and religious Jews might have been horrified by Jesus's treatment of Matthew? According to Matthew 9:11, how did they respond?

_____

_____

_____

Why do you think we feel threatened by spending time with "sinners"? What do we expect will happen to us as a result?

_____

_____

_____

_____

In Matthew 9:12–13, how did Jesus describe the people He chose to spend time with? Did He condemn them for their condition? Why, or why not?

_____

_____

_____

_____

_____

Notice that Jesus never glossed over sin. He didn't rationalize it or ignore it. He called a "sinner" a "sinner." But He never stopped at the sin; He always saw beyond it, through the dirty consequences, to the broken, scarred heart underneath.

In Matthew 9:13, Jesus, quoting Hosea 6:6, challenged the Pharisees in terms that they understood: the Old Testament Law. As a real-life illustration of His relationship with the people of Israel, God told the prophet Hosea to marry a prostitute. She broke Hosea's heart time and time again—leaving home, wallowing in infidelity, and never returning her husband's love. And yet the theme of the whole book of Hosea is God's compassion for Israel, viewed through Hosea's commitment to his wife even when she continually betrayed him.

With this context in mind, what was Jesus's reasoning for His actions?

_____

_____

_____

_____

_____

Using the concordance in the back of your Bible, look up other places where the word *compassion* is used in Scripture. Choose two or three verses and paraphrase them below.

_____

_____

_____

_____

When you are confronted with someone who is involved in a particular sin, is it more natural for you to respond with compassion or judgment? Why?

_____

_____

_____

_____

Jesus never kept Himself apart from unbelievers and sinners in the name of preserving the appearance of His own morality. He dove right into the middle of their lives, never tolerating their sin but always targeting their hearts with passionate grace and forgiveness.

Judgment of Sinners by Sinners

In our culture, we are surrounded by an easy acceptance of sexual immorality. More than half of Americans believe that cohabitation and sexual fantasizing are morally acceptable. Nearly half condone having a sexual relationship with someone other than their spouse. And about one-third of the population approves of the use of pornography and homosexual sex.[1] Television shows and movies glorify the idea of romantic love and sexual fulfillment wherever it can be found—inside or outside of marital boundaries. And much of our worth as women is founded in how attractive we are to the opposite sex.

We are pressured to accept or even participate in this immorality in the name of tolerance, even though we know that God calls us to a higher standard. His Word clearly speaks out against these behaviors as sin (see Deuteronomy 5:18; 1 Corinthians 6:18; 1 Thessalonians 4:3–5).

But in our daily lives, we constantly come across people engaging in sexually immoral lifestyles without shame. How should we respond?

 Read John 8:3–11.

In New Testament times the sin of adultery carried a penalty of death by stoning, so two witnesses were required to corroborate the charge. If the woman in John 8 was "caught in the act" of adultery, whom do you think the witnesses were?

_____

_____

_____

_____

_____

Read verses 5 and 6. When the religious leaders brought the woman before Jesus, what do you think they were hoping He would say? What exactly were they trying to accomplish?

_____

_____

_____

_____

_____

Place yourself in the woman's position for a moment. What emotions do you think she was experiencing? What thoughts might have flitted through her mind?

_____

_____

_____

_____

Look at John 8:6 once more. Many commentators have speculated about what Jesus was writing in the dirt that day. Did He list the sins of the men standing in the crowd? Did He write the name of a prostitute some of the accusers knew a little too well? Did He write a verse or two from the Torah, perhaps one from the Psalms about forgiveness? Maybe. But in our speculation about what we don't know, we can miss what the text clearly says.

Does Jesus's answer to the accusers in verse 7 suggest that we have no business judging someone else's sin? Why, or why not?

_____

_____

_____

_____

Continue to John 8:7–9. When Jesus answered the Pharisees' accusation, how did they respond?

_____

_____

_____

_____

Read John 5:26–27 and Acts 10:38–43. Why does Jesus have the ultimate authority as our Judge?

_____

_____

_____

_____

After He spoke, Jesus bent down again to write in the dust. Gently, He asked the woman, "Where are your accusers?" (John 8:10 NLT). She was bracing herself for death, expecting the stones to fall at any moment. Can you imagine her surprise and abject wonder when she raised her head to see that they had all walked away? What a moment! Jesus then responded with two simple statements: "I do not condemn you either. Go . . . sin no more" (8:11).

Let that sink in for a moment. The woman was caught in the middle of a sin that should have cost her life, and the only One who truly had the authority and power to judge her offered forgiveness instead. And then He told her to leave the past and her sin behind and start fresh. _He gave her a new life._

When you consider Jesus's actions and words, do you think He tolerated her sin? Why, or why not? What was His primary goal in this situation?

_____

_____

_____

_____

What might be her motivation to obey Jesus's command?

_____

_____

How might your understanding of this passage shape your view of people who are involved in sexual sin? Will you treat them differently? What will be your goal as you interact with individuals who are struggling in this area?

_____

_____

_____

The Depths of Grace

Christians have a reputation for mindless intolerance. We are usually quick to judge anyone and anything we deem to be less than perfect. But, in all fairness, we are sinners too. We fail; we fall. And when we refuse to admit it, we are every bit as hypocritical as others suspect us to be.

Read Luke 7:36–39.

How did Simon the Pharisee describe the woman in verse 39? What can you gather about his opinion of her from his thoughts?

_____

_____

_____

_____

Next, Jesus "answered" Simon's *unspoken* concern: "Simon, I have something to say to you" (Luke 7:40). That must have caught his attention immediately! Jesus continued, "Two men were in debt to a banker. One owed five hundred silver pieces, the other fifty. Neither of them could pay up, and so the banker canceled both debts. Which of the two would be more grateful?" (7:41–42 MSG).

Continue to read the passage as paraphrased in *The Message*:

> Simon answered, "I suppose the one who was forgiven the most."
>
> "That's right," said Jesus. Then turning to the woman, but speaking to Simon, he said, "Do you see this woman? I came to your home; you provided no water for my feet, but she rained tears on my feet and dried them with her hair. You gave me no greeting, but from the time I arrived she hasn't quit kissing my feet. You provided nothing for freshening up, but she has soothed my feet with perfume. Impressive, isn't it? She was forgiven many, many sins, and so she is very, very grateful. If the forgiveness is minimal, the gratitude is minimal." (Luke 7:43–47)

Jesus clearly knew who the woman was and understood the depths of her sin. He also knew Simon's background, the way he lived, and the attitude of his heart. So why do you think He dealt with Simon *first*?

_____

_____

_____

_____

STARTING YOUR JOURNEY
Many of us hold up the apostle Paul as an ideal example of the Christ-follower we aspire to be. Yet, he was once "the worst of sinners." It's a story he declared with deepest gratitude:

Even though I was once a blasphemer and a persecu-
tor and a violent man, I was shown mercy because
I acted in ignorance and unbelief. . . . Here is a
trustworthy saying that deserves full acceptance:
Christ Jesus came into the world to save sinners—of
whom I am the worst. But for that very reason I was
shown mercy so that in me, the worst of sinners,
Christ Jesus might display his unlimited patience as
an example for those who would believe on him and
receive eternal life. (1 Timothy 1:13, 15–16 NIV)

In Luke 7:48, 50, Jesus turned to the woman and said, "Your sins
have been forgiven. . . . Your faith has saved you; go in peace." He
alone has the authority to judge and the power to offer forgiveness.
And the woman responded to His grace with a poignant expression of
deepest gratitude.

**Take a few moments to look inside your own heart. Have you
rationalized away any areas of sin because the world tolerates
them? What are they? We all have them.**

_____

_____

_____

_____

**Ponder the implications of the forgiveness you've been given
through Jesus Christ. Write a brief prayer below, thanking Him
for offering you the precious gift of grace.**

_____

_____

_____

_____

Jesus never let sin go unnoticed. He confronted it with truth at every turn. Our world would label Him as unforgivably, inappropriately intolerant. However, when He interacted with people throughout His ministry, Jesus's love, forgiveness, and grace were the underlying foundation for His every word and deed.

Jesus walked into the dirty places of life, never flinching at the sight of an ugly, sinful heart as He sought to bring cleansing and healing. His heart broke when He witnessed fallenness and its consequences. His grace infuriated the self-righteous, confronted the self-reliant, and removed shame from the self-condemned.

How will you choose to walk the line between love and judgment? Will you stand with a pointed finger and a hardened attitude? Will you run away, afraid you might be tainted by the stench of a diseased soul? Or will you allow your heart to be moved with deep compassion for those caught in the consequences of their sin and show them the way to Jesus with love and grace?

How to Begin a Relationship with God

In a world gone haywire, discouragement can easily set in. And as human beings, our nagging desire for something better leads us to search for answers to the world's problems. That desire may send us to any number of sources, but the only source that offers true satisfaction and solace is Jesus Christ. Only by entering into a relationship with Him will we discover true peace and comfort. Let's look at four vital truths the Scripture reveals.

Our Spiritual Condition: Totally Corrupt

The first truth is rather personal. One look in the mirror of Scripture, and our human condition becomes painfully clear:

> There is none righteous, not even one;
> There is none who understands,
> There is none who seeks for God;
> All have turned aside, together they have become
>   useless;
> There is none who does good,
> There is not even one. (Romans 3:10–12)

We are all sinners through and through—totally corrupt. Now, that doesn't mean we've committed every atrocity known to humankind. We're not as *bad* as we can be, just as *bad off* as we can be. Sin colors all our thoughts, motives, words, and actions.

Look around. Everything around us bears the smudge marks of our sinful nature. Despite our best efforts to create a perfect world, crime statistics continue to soar, divorce rates keep climbing, and families keep crumbling.

119

Something has gone terribly wrong in our society and in ourselves, something deadly. Contrary to how the world would repackage it, "me first" living doesn't equal rugged individuality and freedom; it equals death. As Paul said in his letter to the Romans, "The wages of sin is death" (Romans 6:23)—our emotional and physical death through sin's destructiveness and our spiritual death from God's righteous judgment of our sin. This brings us to the second truth: God's character.

God's Character: Infinitely Holy

How can God judge each of us for a sinful state we were born into? Our total depravity is only half the answer. The other half is God's infinite holiness.

The fact that we know things are not as they should be points us to a standard of goodness beyond ourselves. Our sense of injustice in life on this side of eternity implies a perfect standard of justice beyond our reality. That standard and source is God Himself. And God's standard of holiness contrasts starkly with our sinful condition.

Scripture says that "God is Light, and in Him there is no darkness at all" (1 John 1:5). He is absolutely holy—which creates a problem for us. If He is so pure, how can we who are so impure relate to Him?

Perhaps we could try being better people, try to tilt the balance in favor of our good deeds, or seek out wisdom and knowledge for self-improvement. Throughout history, people have attempted to live up to God's standard by keeping the Ten Commandments or living by their own code of ethics. Unfortunately, no one can come close to satisfying the demands of God's law. Romans 3:20 says, "By the works of the Law no flesh will be justified in His sight; for through the Law comes the knowledge of sin."

Our Need: A Substitute

So here we are: sinners by nature and sinners by choice, trying to pull ourselves up by our own bootstraps and attain a relationship with our holy Creator. But every time we try, we fall flat on our faces. We can't live a good enough life to make up for our sin, because God's standard isn't "good enough"—it's *perfection*. And we can't make amends for the offense our sin has created without dying for it.

Who can get us out of this mess?

If someone could live perfectly, honoring God's law, and would bear sin's death penalty for us—in our place—then we would be saved from our predicament. But is there such a person? Thankfully, yes!

Meet your substitute—*Jesus Christ.* He is the One who took death's place for you!

> [God] made [Jesus Christ] who knew no sin to be sin on our behalf, so that we might become the righteousness of God in Him. (2 Corinthians 5:21)

God's Provision: A Savior

God rescued us by sending His Son, Jesus, to die for our sins on the cross (1 John 4:9–10). Jesus was fully human and fully divine (John 1:1, 18), a truth that ensures His understanding of our weaknesses, His power to forgive, and His ability to bridge the gap between God and us (Romans 5:6–11). In short, we are "justified as a gift by His grace through the redemption which is in Christ Jesus" (3:24). Two words in this verse bear further explanation: *justified* and *redemption.*

Justification is God's act of mercy, in which He declares righteous the believing sinners while we are still in our sinning state. Justification doesn't mean that God *makes* us righteous, so that we never sin again, rather that He *declares* us righteous—much like a judge pardons a guilty criminal. Because Jesus took our sin upon Himself and suffered our judgment on the cross, God forgives our debt and proclaims us PARDONED.

Redemption is Christ's act of paying the complete price to release us from sin's bondage. God sent His Son to bear His wrath for all of our sins—past, present, and future (Romans 3:24–26; 2 Corinthians 5:21). In humble obedience, Christ willingly endured the shame of the cross for our sake (Mark 10:45; Romans 5:6–8; Philippians 2:8). Christ's death satisfied God's righteous demands. He no longer holds our sins against us, because His own Son paid the penalty for them. We are freed from the slave market of sin, never to be enslaved again!

Placing Your Faith in Christ

These four truths describe how God has provided a way to Himself through Jesus Christ. Because the price has been paid in full by God, we must respond to His free gift of eternal life in total faith and confidence in Him to save us. We must step forward into the relationship with God that He has prepared for us—not by doing good works or by being a good person, but by coming to Him just as we are and accepting His justification and redemption by faith.

> For by grace you have been saved through faith;
> and that not of yourselves, it is the gift of God;
> not as a result of works, so that no one may boast.
> (Ephesians 2:8–9)

We accept God's gift of salvation simply by placing our faith in Christ alone for the forgiveness of our sins. Would you like to enter a relationship with your Creator by trusting in Christ as your Savior? If so, here's a simple prayer you can use to express your faith:

Dear God,

I know that my sin has put a barrier between You and me.
Thank You for sending Your Son, Jesus, to die in my place.
I trust in Jesus alone to forgive my sins, and I accept His
gift of eternal life. I ask Jesus to be my personal Savior
and the Lord of my life. Thank You. In Jesus's name I pray,
amen.

If you've prayed this prayer or one like it and you wish to find out more about knowing God and His plan for you in the Bible, contact us at Insight for Living. Our contact information is on the following pages.

We Are Here for You

If you desire to find out more about knowing God and His plan for you in the Bible, contact us. Insight for Living provides staff pastors who are available for free written correspondence or phone consultation. These seminary-trained and seasoned counselors have years of experience and are well-qualified guides for your spiritual journey.

Please feel welcome to contact your regional Pastoral Ministries by using the information below:

United States

Insight for Living
Pastoral Ministries
Post Office Box 269000
Plano, Texas 75026-9000
USA
972-473-5097, Monday through Friday,
8:00 a.m. – 5:00 p.m. Central time
www.insight.org/contactapastor

Canada

Insight for Living Canada
Pastoral Ministries
Post Office Box 2510
Vancouver, BC V6B 3W7
CANADA
1-800-663-7639
info@insightforliving.ca

Australia, New Zealand, and South Pacific

Insight for Living Australia
Pastoral Care
Post Office Box 1011
Bayswater, VIC 3153
AUSTRALIA
1 300 467 444

United Kingdom and Europe

Insight for Living United Kingdom
Pastoral Care
Post Office Box 348
Leatherhead
KT22 2DS
UNITED KINGDOM
0800 915 9364
+44 (0) 1372 370 055
pastoralcare@insightforliving.org.uk

Endnotes

Chapter One

1. David Jeremiah, *What in the World Is Going On?: 10 Prophetic Clues You Cannot Afford to Ignore* (Grand Rapids: Thomas Nelson, 2008), 142–43.

2. Steve Farrar, *Standing Tall: How a Man Can Protect His Family* (Sisters, Ore.: Multnomah, 1994), 18.

3. I have been especially influenced in the area of understanding our world by a book of Wood Kroll's called *Back to the Bible: Turning Your Life Around with God's Word* (Sisters, Ore.: Multnomah, 2000). I'd encourage you to read it as you deepen your understanding of our times.

4. Kroll, *Back to the Bible*, 134.

5. Gary M. Burge, "The Greatest Story Never Read: Recovering Biblical Literacy in the Church," in *Christianity Today*, August 9, 1999, http://www.christianitytoday.com/ct/1999/august9/9t9045.html (accessed March 19, 2009).

6. Vaclav Havel, "The Need for Transcendence in the Postmodern World," *The Futurist* 29 (1995): 47.

7. Kroll, *Back to the Bible*, 84.

8. Francis A. Schaeffer, *The Great Evangelical Disaster* (Westchester, Ill.: Crossway, 1984), 37.

9. Kroll, *Back to the Bible*, 84–88.

Chapter Two

1. Frederick William Danker, ed., *A Greek-English Lexicon of the New Testament and Other Early Christian Literature*, 3d ed. (Chicago: University of Chicago Press, 2000), 1054.

2. John Calvin, *Commentaries on the Catholic Epistles* (Grand Rapids: Eerdmans, 1948), 192.

3. John R. W. Stott, *The Letters of John: An Introduction and Commentary*, 2d ed. (Grand Rapids: Eerdmans, 1988), 117–18.

4. Wayne W. Dyer, *Your Sacred Self: Making the Decision to Be Free* (New York: HarperCollins/Quill, 1995), x.

5. Erwin W. Lutzer, *Ten Lies about God: And How You May Already Be Deceived* (Nashville: Word, 2000), 26.

6. Charles Colson, *A Dance with Deception: Revealing the Truth Behind the Headlines* (Dallas: Word, 1993), 277.

Chapter Three

1. Leslie Pepper, "A Parents Guide to Teens Behaving Badly," in *Family Circle*, April 17, 2009, 54.

2. Lloyd John Ogilvie, *Facing the Future Without Fear: Prescriptions for Courageous Living in the New Millennium* (Ann Arbor: Vine Books, 1999), 28.

Chapter Four

1. Ray Johnston, *Developing Spiritual Growth in Junior High Students* (El Cajon, Calif.: Youth Specialties, 1994), 24.

2. Marshall Shelley and Larry Weeden, "Can Spiritual Maturity Be Taught? An Interview with Roberta Hestenes," *Leadership Journal.net*, October 1, 1988, http://www.christianitytoday.com/le/1988/fall/88l4012.html?start=1 (accessed April 30, 2009).

3. Junior Achievement, "Junior Achievement's 2008 Teen Holiday Spending Poll," http://www.ja.org/files/polls/holiday_spending_2008.pdf (accessed April 29, 2009).

4. Douglas Rushkoff, "The Merchants of Cool," *Frontline*, PBS WGBH Boston, Feb. 27, 2001, http://www.pbs.org/wgbh/pages/frontline/shows/cool/ (accessed April 30, 2009).

5. *Merriam-Webster's Collegiate Dictionary*, 11th ed. (Springfield, Mass.: Merriam-Webster, 2007), see "absolute."

6. Sid S. Buzzell, "Proverbs," in *The Bible Knowledge Commentary: Old Testament*, ed. John F. Walvoord and Roy B. Zuck (Wheaton, Ill.: Victor Books, 1986), 902.

Chapter Six

1. See Lauren F. Winner, *Real Sex: The Naked Truth about Chastity* (Grand Rapids: Brazos Press, 2006).

2. The Barna Group, "American Lifestyles Mix Compassion and Self-Oriented Behavior," February 5, 2007, http://www.barna.org/barna-update/article/20-donorscause/110-american-lifestyles-mix-compassion-and-self-oriented-behavior (accessed May 4, 2009).

3. David Kinnaman and Gabe Lyons, *UnChristian: What a New Generation Really Thinks about Christianity . . . and Why it Matters*, (Grand Rapids: Baker Books, 2007), 54. Based on a study by the Barna Group "A New Generation Bends Moral and Sexual Rules to Their Liking," October 31, 2006, http://www.barna.org/barna-update/article/13-culture/144-a-new-generation-of-adults-bends-moral-and-sexual-rules-to-their-liking (accessed May 4, 2009).

4. Kinnaman and Lyons, *UnChristian*, 49.

Chapter Eight

1. John N. Oswalt, "batach," in *Theological Wordbook of the Old Testament*, vol. 1, ed. R. Laird Harris, Gleason L. Archer, and Bruce K. Waltke (Chicago: Moody, 1980), 101.

2. Ralph H. Alexander, "yada," in *Theological Wordbook of the Old Testament*, 364–65.

3. Francis Brown, S. R. Driver, and Charles A. Briggs, eds., *The New Brown-Driver-Briggs-Gesenius Hebrew and English Lexicon* (Peabody, Mass.: Hendrickson, 1979), 448.

Chapter Nine

1. The Barna Group, "Morality Continues to Decay," November 3, 2003, http://barna.org/barna-update/article/5-barna-update/129-morality-continues-to-decay (accessed April 8, 2009).

Resources for Probing Further

For further information on how to manage in these troubled times, here are a few resources we would like to recommend. Of course, we cannot always endorse everything a writer or ministry says, so we encourage you to approach these and all other nonbiblical resources with wisdom and discernment.

CHAPTER 1–2

Kroll, Wood. *Back to the Bible: Turning Your Life Around with God's Word*. Sisters, Ore.: Multnomah, 2000.

CHAPTER 3: PRETEENS

Barna, George. *Revolutionary Parenting*. Carol Stream, Ill.: BarnaBooks, 2007.

Biehl, Bobb. *The On My Own Handbook: 100 Secrets of Success to Prepare Young People for Life*. Colorado Springs: Victor Books, 1997.

Dobson, James C. *The New Strong-Willed Child*. Rev. ed. of *The Strong-Willed Child*. Wheaton, Ill.: Tyndale House, 2007.

Leman, Kevin. *Have a New Kid by Friday: How to Change Your Child's Attitude, Behavior and Character in 5 Days*. Grand Rapids: Revell, 2008.

Swindoll, Charles R. *Parenting: From Surviving to Thriving*. Nashville: Thomas Nelson, 2006.

Swindoll, Charles R. *The Strong Family*. Grand Rapids: Zondervan, 1991.

www.cpyu.org
The Web site for The Center for Parent-Youth Understanding.

CHAPTER 4: MIDDLE SCHOOL

Clark, Chap. *Hurt: Inside the World of Today's Teenagers*. Grand Rapids: Baker Books, 2004.

Dobson, James C. *The New Strong-Willed Child*. Rev. ed. of *The Strong-Willed Child*. Wheaton, Ill.: Tyndale House, 2007.

Elkind, David. *All Grown Up and No Place to Go: Teenagers in Crisis*. Rev. ed. New York: Perseus Books, 1998.

Kimmel, Tim. *Why Christian Kids Rebel: Trading Heartache for Hope*. Nashville: Thomas Nelson, 2004.

McDowell, Josh. *Evidence for Christianity*. Nashville: Thomas Nelson, 2006.

Rice, Wayne. *Enjoy Your Middle Schooler: A Guide to Understanding the Physical, Social, Emotional, and Spiritual Changes of Your 11–14 Year Old*. Grand Rapids: Zondervan, 1994.

Rice, Wayne. *Junior High Ministry: A Guide to Early Adolescence for Youth Workers*. Grand Rapids: Zondervan, 1998.

Swindoll, Charles R. *Parenting: From Surviving to Thriving*. Nashville: Thomas Nelson, 2006.

Swindoll, Charles R. *The Strong Family*. Grand Rapids: Zondervan, 1991.

www.cpyu.org
The Web site for The Center for Parent-Youth Understanding.

www.pbs.org/wgbh/pages/frontline/shows/cool/
This Web site features "The Merchants of Cool," a documentary on youth culture done for *Frontline* in 2001.

www.planetwisdom.com
The Web site of Mark Matlock; this site provides excellent material for youth, especially on the book of Proverbs.

www.thesource4ym.com
   The Web site for The Source for Youth Ministry; this site offers insights on teen culture.

CHAPTER 5: HIGH SCHOOL

Dobson, James C. *The New Strong-Willed Child*. Rev. ed. of *The Strong-Willed Child*. Wheaton, Ill.: Tyndale House, 2007.

Elkind, David. *All Grown Up and No Place to Go: Teenagers in Crisis*. Rev. ed. New York: Perseus Books, 1998.

Kimmel, Tim. *Why Christian Kids Rebel: Trading Heartache for Hope*. Nashville: Thomas Nelson, 2004.

McDowell, Josh. *Evidence for Christianity*. Nashville: Thomas Nelson, 2006.

Strobel, Lee. *The Case for Faith: A Journalist Investigates the Toughest Objections to Christianity*. Grand Rapids: Zondervan, 2000.

Swindoll, Charles R. *Parenting: From Surviving to Thriving*. Nashville: Thomas Nelson, 2006.

Swindoll, Charles R. *The Strong Family*. Grand Rapids: Zondervan, 1991.

www.cpyu.org
   The Web site for The Center for Parent-Youth Understanding.

CHAPTER 6: SINGLES

Allender, Dan B. *Leading with a Limp*. Colorado Springs: WaterBrook Press, 2006.

Anderson, J. Kerby. *Moral Dilemmas: Biblical Perspectives on Contemporary Ethical Issues*. Nashville: W Publishing, 1998.

Kinnaman, David, and Gabe Lyons. *Unchristian: What a New Generation Really Thinks about Christianity . . . and Why It Matters*. Grand Rapids: Baker Books, 2007.

www.probe.org
 The mission of Probe Ministries is to present the gospel to communities, nationally and internationally, by providing lifelong opportunities to integrate faith and learning through balanced, biblically based scholarship, training people to love God by renewing their minds and equipping the church to engage the world for Christ.

CHAPTER 7: MARRIEDS

Dobson, James C. *Love for a Lifetime: Building a Marriage That Will Go the Distance*. Portland, Ore.: Multnomah, 2004.

Rainey, Dennis, and Barbara Rainey. *Starting Your Marriage Right: What You Need to Know and Do in the Early Years to Make It Last a Lifetime*. Nashville: Thomas Nelson, 2007.

Swindoll, Charles R. *Marriage: From Surviving to Thriving*. Nashville: Thomas Nelson, 2006.

CHAPTER 8: MEN

Farrar, Steve. *How to Ruin Your Life by 40*. Chicago: Moody Publishers, 2006.

Hughes, R. Kent. *Disciplines of a Godly Man*. Wheaton, Ill.: Crossway Books, 2006.

Swindoll, Charles R. *Man to Man*. Grand Rapids: Zondervan, 1996.

www.cbmw.org
 The Web site for The Council on Biblical Manhood and Womanhood.

www.fathers.com
 The Web site of the National Center for Fathering; this site is dedicated to helping men become better dads.

www.stevefarrar.com
 The Web site of author Steve Farrar; he is founder and chairman of Men's Leadership Ministries.

CHAPTER 9: WOMEN

Barna, George. *Think Like Jesus: Make the Right Decision Every Time.* Nashville: Thomas Nelson, 2005.

Ferguson, David. *The Never Alone Church.* Wheaton, Ill.: Tyndale House, 2002.

Kinnaman, David, and Gabe Lyons. *Unchristian: What a New Generation Really Thinks about Christianity . . . and Why It Matters.* Grand Rapids: Baker Books, 2007.

Swindoll, Charles R. *The Grace Awakening.* Nashville: Thomas Nelson, 2006.

www.cbmw.org
The Web site for The Council on Biblical Manhood and Womanhood.

About the Authors

Charles R. Swindoll

Best-selling author Chuck Swindoll serves as senior pastor of Stonebriar Community Church in Frisco, Texas, where he's able to do what he loves most — teach the Bible to willing hearts. He also serves as chancellor and adjunct professor for Doctor of Ministry Studies at Dallas Theological Seminary. His focus on practical Bible application has been heard on the *Insight for Living* radio broadcast since 1979.

David Ake

David Ake received his bachelor's degree from the University of Texas-Pan American and his master's degree in Biblical Studies from Dallas Theological Seminary. He currently serves as pastor of Junior High Ministries at Stonebriar Community Church. David, his wife, Jamie, and their two children reside in Frisco, Texas.

Terry Boyle

Terry Boyle was born in Windsor, England. Although he began his professional life as a biochemist, Terry earned a Master of Theology degree from Dallas Theological Seminary in 1999 and is presently a candidate for a Ph.D. in Bible Exposition. He served as senior pastor of Skillman Bible Church in Dallas until he and his family moved back to the United Kingdom in 2007 to take on the role of the pastor for Insight for Living United Kingdom. Terry and his wife, Rose, have three children: Hannah, Emily, and Terence.

Tony Cammarota

Tony Cammarota serves as pastor of Equipping Ministries at
Stonebriar Community Church in Frisco, Texas. A graduate of
Dallas Theological Seminary, he holds a Master of Theology degree in
New Testament Studies and Pastoral Leadership. He has been married
for eleven years to Dorianne and is the father of four. Tony's desire
is to authentically live out the gospel before others and to encourage
Christians to do the same.

Brianna Barrier Engeler

Brianna Barrier Engeler is a graduate of Baylor University and
Dallas Theological Seminary. Out of her deep passion for communi-
cating biblical truth, she served on the staff of Insight for Living for
four years. Brie is now a busy freelance writer, editor, and conference
speaker, working with a variety of churches and ministries across the
country. Brie and her husband, Derrek, live in sunny Destin, Florida.

Les Fleetwood

A charter member of Stonebriar Community Church in Frisco, Texas,
Les Fleetwood serves as pastor of Connecting and Equipping
Ministries. After four years of itinerant evangelism in Canada, the
United States, Mexico, and Guatemala, Les pursued a degree at
Dallas Theological Seminary, earning his Master of Theology in
Educational Leadership and Family Ministry. His mission is to encour-
age others to pursue a lifelong, joyous relationship with Jesus Christ
by providing opportunities for their spiritual growth and authentic
community. Les and Nidelvia have been married since 1989 and
reside in McKinney, Texas.

Joe Harms

Joe Harms currently serves as the associate pastor of Preteen
Ministries at Stonebriar Community Church in Frisco, Texas.
This year Joe celebrates thirty-three years of marriage to his wife,
Christine, and they are the proud parents of Justin (28), Wendy
(26), and Zach (22). Prior to serving at Stonebriar, Joe spent nine
years with International Community School in Bangkok, Thailand,
serving as both a teacher and an administrator. He received his
bachelor's degrees in Christian Education and Secondary Education
from Grace University in Omaha and from the University of Nebraska
at Omaha. He also earned a master's degree in Educational Leadership
from the University of Northern Arizona. Joe loves to play any sport
involving a ball of some type, and he loves teaching preteens!

Jason Stevenson

Jason Stevenson is the pastor of Student Ministries and High School
Ministries at Stonebriar Community Church in Frisco, Texas. He
received his master's degree in Christian Education from Dallas
Theological Seminary and has a bachelor's degree in Secondary
Education. He has been continuously involved in various programs
and ministries to teenagers, including camps, teaching, and youth
ministry, since 1989. Jason lives in the Dallas area with his wife,
Carley, and a son.

Ordering Information

If you would like to order additional copies of *Hope for Our Troubled Times* or order other Insight for Living resources, please contact the office that serves you.

United States

Insight for Living
Post Office Box 269000
Plano, Texas 75026-9000
USA
1-800-772-8888
Monday through Friday,
7:00 a.m.–7:00 p.m.
Central time
www.insight.org
www.insightworld.org

Canada

Insight for Living Canada
Post Office Box 2510
Vancouver, BC V6B 3W7
CANADA
1-800-663-7639
www.insightforliving.ca

Australia, New Zealand, and South Pacific

Insight for Living Australia
Post Office Box 1011
Bayswater, VIC 3153
AUSTRALIA
1 300 467 444
www.insight.asn.au

United Kingdom and Europe

Insight for Living United Kingdom
Post Office Box 348
Leatherhead
KT22 2DS
UNITED KINGDOM
0800 915 9364
www.insightforliving.org.uk

Other International Locations

International constituents may contact the U.S. office through our Web site (www.insightworld.org), mail queries, or by calling +1-972-473-5136.

Notes

Notes